Vocal Yokel

By the Same Author

The Benefits Racket
Down Among the Dossers
The Decline of an English Village
The Hunter and the Hunted
Weather-forecasting the Country Way
Cures and Remedies the Country Way
Animal Cures the Country Way
Weeds the Country Way
The Journal of a Country Parish
Journeys into Britain
The Country Way of Love
The Wildlife of the Royal Estates
A Fox's Tale
The Fox and the Orchid
Dust in a Dark Continent (Africa)
Gardening the Country Way
A Peasant's Diary
Gone to the Dogs

Children's Books
How the Fox got its Pointed Nose
How the Heron got Long Legs

Vocal Yokel

Robin Page

EXCELLENT PRESS

Excellent Press
Metro House
5 Eastman Road
Acton
London W3 7YG

First published in the UK by Excellent Press, 1996

A copy of the British Library Cataloguing in Publication Data for this title
is available from the British Library.

ISBN 1 900318 03 2

Typeset by Dorwyn Ltd, Rowlands Castle, Hants
Printed and bound in the EC

Dedication

۶ىL

To all country people who are proud of their culture, traditions and inheritance. Also to those many townspeople who are happy to share in, and respect, our rural customs and values.

Contents

ह्र

Preface

❧

I did not expect to be writing another introduction to a collection of assorted writings and musings at this time. The truth is that the previous two, *A Peasant's Diary* and *Gone to the Dogs* sold out so quickly that a third became inevitable. It has come at an interesting time; pressure on rural values and communities is increasing; change in the countryside is almost out of control and more and more people and politicians seem to regard rural Britain as little more than a theme park. But at last country people are beginning to fight back. The yokels are becoming vocal; the natives are restless and we hope that people will at last begin to listen.

Movements and organisations are starting to spring up defending country ways and traditions. Who knows, soon we even may get one or two real rural MPs defending the countryside in Parliament. It is ironic, at the time of a *A Peasant's Diary* Edwina Currie (see 'A Yokel's Who's Who') , then Health Minister, had ruined many small egg-producing farmers through absurd comments and actions related to Salmonella. As I write, a similar fiasco is taking place with beef and 'mad cows'; thousands of cows are being slaughtered for no good reason and numerous family farms are being put out of business through a mixture of ignorance, incompetence and political expediency.

Consequently over the last two years I have had much to write about: a great deal of it has been good, beautiful, humorous and positive, but as usual there has also been much hypocritical nonsense and fantasy to contend with as people who do not understand the countryside try to run it.

I am grateful to *The Daily Telegraph* for permission to reproduce so many of the articles I first wrote for them and also the *Field*, the *Shooting Times*, *Heritage*, *Country Living* and the *Eastern Daily Press* for allowing me to use articles I first wrote for them.

I am grateful to my family for putting up with my many foibles while putting the whole thing together and to Margaret Taylor for typing some of the manuscript. I must thank my publisher David Burnett too. As some companies go out of country books, he has kept faith with the tradition of country writing and we should all be grateful to him for that.

During the time it has taken for this book to form I have continued working as Chairman of the Countryside Restoration Trust. In just three years we have grown from 0 to 3000 'Friends of the Countryside'; from £0 to £280,000; from 0 acres to 40 acres; from little wildlife, to much wildlife; from accepting the industrialisation of farming and the countryside, to trying to stop it and getting the 'culture' back into agri-CULTURE. We are trying to encourage profitable farming with attractive landscapes and abundant wildlife; we want farmers to work with nature, not against it; we want animals treated with humanity and respect, we want thriving rural communities with money coming from the land, and we want skylarks singing again over every field. If you enjoy this book, or at least agree with parts of it, please join us. Details of the Countryside Restoration Trust can be obtained from: The CRT, Barton, Cambridgeshire, CB3 7AG. The countryside needs all the help and the 'friends' it can get.

1

What a Hoot

೭ᗒ

I nearly drove off the road the other night. My problem was not that I was driving without due care and attention: I was driving with too much care and attention, care and attention for owls. As I drive during dusk and darkness I have got into the habit of looking at the top of telegraph poles for little owls and scanning fence posts and verges for barn owls. It was a barn owl on – and off – a fence post that caught my eye. What made it so exciting for me was the fact that it was on the outskirts of my own village, the first barn owl I had seen in my parish since 1963.

The 'white owl', the familiar and much loved owl of my child-hood, simply dropped from the fence post into a clump of long grass, then flew back up to the post top, complete with mouse or vole in large, sharp talons. I should explain, for all those who enjoy soya burgers, the barn owl is not a vegetarian. I felt happier than if I had won the lottery, for barn owls hunting, feeding and breeding in the parish once again, would be a price of far greater value than simple money.

My elation was somewhat tempered by the fact that the barn owl was perching close to Junction 12 of the M11 and 54% of all barn owl mortalities are road casualties. I wonder when car advertisements are going to reflect the annual wildlife carnage on our roads, and when are vehicle manufacturers going to persuade drivers to drive slower through the countryside;

instead of encouraging them to seek speed, fast corners and burning rubber, leaving a trail of splattered, shattered birds, bees and animals in their wake?

The current slow but steady increase in barn owl numbers is one of the few good results of set-aside. But sadly in many areas the owls are trying to return to a countryside devoid of suitable old barns, buildings and trees in which to nest. Thirty-three years is a long time in over-populated, agriculturally ravaged, car-dominated rural Britain.

In the hope that this one barn owl has friends in the area the Hawk and Owl Trust has presented the Countryside Restoration Trust with a number of barn owl boxes, as well as couple of kestrel boxes. We are erecting them in old willow trees by the brook, on the Trust's 40 acres, and we will wait to see what happens. They are posh, complete with pitched roofs and inspection hatches.

If no occupants arrive we will attempt a properly monitored barn owl introduction programme, as there now appears to be plenty of suitable habitat for them. Much will depend on the attitude of the environmentally illiterate Cambridgeshire County Council; at key areas we will want signs urging drivers to drive slower, for the sake of owls and otters. I expect Cambs CC will plead a shortage of cash, although money always seems to be available to fill the countryside up with street lights, encouraging motorists to drive still faster.

Indeed, one set of incredibly ugly lights, near Junction 12 of the M11, owl country, seems architecturally in keeping with Milton Keynes, not the open fields. Why are so many unwanted urban intrusions being forced into virtually every aspect of our country lives?

It is the intention of the Countryside Restoration Trust to work as closely as possible with other Trusts and organisations. We hope to complement their activities, not compete with them. Because of this, Colin Shawyer of the Hawk and Owl Trust has seen our land and our work and has been very positive and helpful.

One of his suggestions came as a body blow to both me and the redoubtable Badger. 'Stop hedge-laying there,' he said, as he surveyed Badger's skilful handiwork. He explained that as barn owls hunt, they tend to travel along the lowest contour. As a result, if we ever get them permanently back, they will move backwards and forwards through our low-lying clay valley, along the line of the brook. We were cutting and laying the hedge down towards the brook, and so eventually, if and when we finish the job, at the lowest point where hedge meets water, the level of the adjoining road will be higher than the hedge. Any passing barn owls will then become part of the 54% statistics for road casualties. 'At that point', Colin Shawyer said, 'you want to be growing the hedge as high as possible, to force any barn owl up and over the road in safety.' Like so many things in conservation it was obvious, once it had been explained. We were glad our folly had been spotted. If only other farmers would open their eyes, and their minds, to the often little things they are doing that can be so destructive. Now it will be a rule on the farm, and on the Trust meadows: low land, high hedges, safe owls. As a result, our next day's hedging will be going up-hill.

John Green, the 'otter man' of the local wildlife trust has been equally helpful. On the CRT's island, we recently built a brand new otter holt out of lengths of freshly cut willow. For extra warmth and dryness, we lined the roof with plastic dustbin bags; it seemed common sense. This was wrong, too; plastic does keep dampness out, but it also keeps it in, causing mould and mildew. So the holt has been dismantled and rebuilt without plastic, to the future satisfaction of the otters, we hope. It is good being an ignorant peasant, it makes learning so interesting. It will only be by thinking, watching, listening and learning that much of the general countryside's wildlife will be saved.

2

Spare Rib

In this chapter I wanted to tell a very funny, true story; alas I cannot – it hurts too much when I laugh. My self-diagnosis suggests a cracked rib, sustained when I became stuck between two large Australians. The first was a well-built Murray Grey, one of our cows, going backwards. The second was a large bulging bicepted colonial, a real Australian, going forwards. I was the human sandwich in the middle of this meeting of muscle, thankyou very much, and my rib was not impressed.

We were testing our cow herd for brucellosis and TB. In the old days when we were dairy, with Friesians, testing days were no real problem. Now we have a beef herd, with Murray Greys, the performance is a nightmare. Unfortunately Australian cows behave like stereotyped Australian people; what coming from Down-Under does to Australian cricketers and rugby players, it does to Clover and Clematis as well.

My problem started straightaway. Heaving the first cow the final foot into the cattle crush with my back, life suddenly became warm and steaming from the neck downwards. Unfortunately at this time of year the consistency of a cow-pat can be likened to that of Yorkshire pudding mixture; a substance not to be encountered at close range.

The second cow coughed while running and shot digested grass from its rear end at me from five feet, like a gun, scoring a direct hit down my front. Why the vet could not have come at the end of August when cow pat manufacture is drier and coarser, we were not told.

The third beast trod on my foot; the fourth deposited more of the green, warm material into my left wellington boot. So already dripping front and back, squelching and limping, by the time I was caught in the Australian pincer movement, I was beyond caring. Surely it is time for the Animal Liberation Front to start demonstrating on my behalf, to save me from any further stress, damage or disorder?

The last cow to be driven into the 'crush' is always the worst. This time the lunatic lady jumped onto the bonnet of our tractor, parked to keep the cattle near the crush, and rejoined the herd. From an almost standing start she landed spreadeagled over the tractor, with her body weight squirting milk from her udder in four directions at once – it was an incredible feat. If only cows could be raced at Aintree, we would have a winner. I wish I could persuade my brother to have a calmer, more traditional breed of cow; I really fancy a return to the Red Poll or Beef Shorthorn.

After the rodeo I did not go to the doctor's with my rib, as I know the treatment from days gone by. It is simple: do not laugh, cough or sneeze. Sadly, with the Labour leadership battle in full cry and the air full of pollen, I am doing all three at regular intervals.

We do not test the cattle for our own amusement. It is to keep our herd disease free at MAAF's command. It is a pity that MAAF was not so disease conscious when it allowed food made from sheep with scrapie to be fed to cattle. Common sense says that feeding diseased meat to herbivores is unnatural and dangerous and so the resulting BSE, Bovine Spongiform Encephalopathy, should have surprised no one. The fact that the Germans and French want to ban our beef should surprise no-one either; if the boot was on the other foot we would take exactly the same position. Interestingly, although British officialdom claims that there are no links between BSE and

8

Creutzfeldt-Jacob disease (CJD) in humans, as I understand it, several researchers involved in studying scrapie have developed CJD and there is much informed scientific opinion that takes the next step and links BSE with CJD. MAAF officials take a different view; they would, wouldn't they, because if ever BSE and CJD are definitely linked, then it is MAAF that will rightly carry the can.

The one member of our cattle herd not tested was Zebbeddee the bull; he was on a working holiday in the Fens. He made his first journey out there a year ago. Then it took four people to drive him into the back of the cattle lorry, with much sweat, tears and frustration. We were expecting a repeat performance this year, but as soon as Zebbeddee heard the lorry his ears twitched; on seeing it he bellowed and when the back was down he literally skipped on board. Alas Zebbeddee has retained yet another unfortunate Australian trait.

I do not want to shop by television; I do not want any more phone lines and I certainly have no desire for any more junk television. Yet despite this Cambridge Cable have just laid their infernal cable outside my house, digging through the roots of several of my trees as they went. To get to me they dug their way noisily past several hedges at peak bird breeding time: apparently bird protection laws do not protect birds from cable layers. They then dug their way through my neighbours' daffodil patch, before reaching my parent's farmhouse, a listed building in a Conservation Area. There, the cable layers announced that they were to erect a large plastic junction box on the verge. Apparently Conservation Areas, listed buildings, tree roots and nesting birds are of little concern to cable companies; they can do virtually what they like, when they like, where they like. So what is the point of having environmental protection laws and Conservation regulations when some individuals can quite legally ignore them completely? It does show that the conservation convictions of our politicians are extremely flimsy and superficial.

The cablers kindly gave us the size of the junction box in centimetres, a foreign language. My sister asked for the information in feet and inches, they didn't know, they would get back to us; we are still waiting. Ouch. I have just discovered that my rib also hurts when I sigh, in exasperation.

3

For We Like Sheep

&

Some people believe that the wealth of Britain, both social and economic, was not built on the industrial revolution, the Empire, or coal, but on sheep, for wool, meat and breeding. Most parts of the country have a tradition of sheep; indeed it is now widely believed that in some of our highland areas there are in fact too many sheep, leading to over grazing and even erosion.

The sight, sound and smell of sheep invariably conjures up pictures of green fields, leafy lanes, rolling downland and distant mountain sides. There is a feeling of deep country with the bleating of sheep caught on the breeze along with the call of larks, lapwings and a plaintive curlew. Then comes a sudden whistle; it is the shepherd and his dog as they drive the flock to pastures new.

The job of shepherding has a romantic ring. Shepherds are usually real countrymen who understand their flocks through a mixture of experience and a feel for their animals. Most read the weather signs like a simple picture book and the bond of trust and affection that develops between a shepherd and his dog is deep, important and lasting. It was because of all these things: beauty, tradition, deepest countryside and skilled, humble men working with their dogs and sheep that I jumped at the opportunity of presenting 'One Man and His Dog' on television, when Phil Drabble retired last year. It was a wise decision as the series, filmed in the Lake District, was a total pleasure to be involved with.

Of course, there is more to shepherding than simply the shepherd and his sheep. Craftsmanship and skill often went into the making of the crooks, sticks and hurdles, and in the sheep bells that were once commonly used in southern England. The sound of the bell kept the shepherd in touch with his sheep; he knew where and when they were in the next valley. The old lanterns could also be small works of art. One still hangs in our old stable, with skilled metal work and 'windows' of thinly sliced ram's horn.

Gordon Beningfield has a wonderful collection of old shepherding artefacts in his home – bells and crooks and an old shepherd's chair made of wood. In his garden a Victorian shepherd's hut stands in the trees, like an antique railway wagon on wheels. The shepherds would eat, sleep and live in their huts at lambing time to ensure the welfare of their flocks.

The sheep themselves must not be forgotten in all this, because the old agricultural improvers have given Britain a rich variety of regional breeds from the Herdwick, Leicester Long-wool, Welsh Mountain, Romney Marsh, Suffolk and many more.

I have only had sheep on our small farm for about five years, but already I am won over. The learning process has been fascinating, rewarding, frustrating, ·heart-rending and heart-warming, and is still going on. It will be several more years before I can call myself a proper shepherd.

Now is the time that the ram is put in with the ewes. I have gone in for traditional, sensible shepherding, with my lambs being born in the spring. I borrow a ram, Tom the Texel, from up the road. His owner went out of sheep several years ago, but hung on to his pedigree ram. Now, each autumn I collect him for a working holiday and put the coloured harness on him – the raddle – so that he marks each ewe when he says 'Good Morning' to her in amorous fashion.

Last year as we arrived at the field, the side door of the trailer flew open and Tom stood there surveying the scene and sniffing the air – if painted he would have been 'Tom – Monarch of the Fen'. Suddenly he leapt – he flew – he landed – he crashed – ending up with his nose against the electric fence. As a blue spark rushed up his left nostril he appeared to attempt a spectacular backward somersault. Perhaps I should give him the electric treatment every year, for that night he said 'Good morning' to six members of his harem. An elderly shepherd in Hertfordshire is not impressed at this figure: 'That's nothing. I had one old ram that managed twenty-four in his first night'. I bet he made some of the toughest mutton ever tasted.

Once Tom is with the flock I walk across the fields to check their welfare every evening as the sun begins to set. It is then that I feel that I am helping to keep the old tradition of shepherding alive – a tradition that spreads back into history for well over 2000 years. As I approach, one of my ewes always shows her appreciation. She jumps over the fence and comes trotting along to meet me. With the western sky still glowing red and stars lighting up the darkening sky – it feels like frost. An owl calls and Bramble my dog trots faithfully at my heels. I feel so grateful to be alive, in the country – in reality.

4

Banned For Being a Bounder

૨ટ

I have recently had a shock. Over the last 12 months I have been invited to speak at various conservation meetings all over the country. Evidently the theme of farming with wildlife and attractive landscapes, promoted through this column, has struck a chord nationwide – well, not quite nationwide; apparently not in Suffolk, where I have been *banned*!

Way back in April I was invited to speak at the Sudbury Group of the Suffolk Wildlife Trust; not unsurprisingly they wanted me to talk about 'Farming and Wildlife'. Like most of East Anglia, Suffolk has its good farmers, but it also has its share of absolute plonkers. Indeed I was driving along a Suffolk road the other day, where not only had the farmer removed the hedges on both sides of the road, he was also ploughing the verge, almost up to the carriageway itself. Because of examples like this, I willingly accepted the invitation. Then, a few weeks before the talk was due, without any prior warning, I received a letter from the Director of the Suffolk Wildlife Trust simply saying: 'You had been booked by our Sudbury Members Group to give a talk on September 27th 1995. I am sorry to advise you that this event has been cancelled. I apologise for any inconvenience caused'. How odd.

Several phone calls then followed from ordinary SWT members, apologising for the Director's directive. Apparently, I had been summarily banned for being politically incorrect and conservationally impure. My sin, it seems, was that I believe in the sensible control of magpies, foxes and crows – a subject that I usually cover in my talks in about two sentences. Evidently two sentences on such a subject in Suffolk amounts to a crime. In disbelief I phoned the Director; if I understood him correctly, yes I had been banned for advocating the control of predators – foxes, crows and magpies. According to Mr Director I also believe in controlling birds of prey.

This is all very strange. Most practical conservationists, and conservation organisations now advocate controlling magpies, crows and foxes where they are known to pose a threat to vulnerable species. But birds of prey? I have actively been working with the Hawk and Owl Trust around the farm and on the CRT land. We have erected Barn Owl and kestrel boxes, and hope to add boxes for little owls and baskets for hobbys. In the past all I have said is, that if a vulnerable species is being made even more vulnerable by birds of prey – those individual troublemakers should be disturbed, disrupted or removed under licence. I had in mind a pair of sparrowhawks specialising in snipe at the Ouse Washes, and that notorious peregrine falcon that almost single-wingedly drove Britain's last remaining roseate terns to Ireland. What, from a responsible conservation viewpoint, is wrong with that?

Interestingly, some time ago the Suffolk Director wrote to a *Telegraph* reader about predators and predation. He wrote: 'The

numbers of any predator are entirely governed by the prey species available'. How quaint. In days gone by this was probably true; in modern Britain it is utter tosh. Foxes, magpies and crows are currently all experiencing population booms quite unrelated to the availability of 'prey species'. In winter they are being kept alive by eating wildlife road casualties, food put out for cattle and sheep and the contents of millions of bird tables. Then in spring, with the populations of all three higher than ever before, they hoover up the eggs and young of ground-nesting birds, before the magpies and crows set about the songbirds.

In addition, there are more birds of prey surviving the winter, too. Sparrowhawks are kept fit and healthy by the unnaturally high populations of tits around bird tables making the bird table the equivalent of a sparrowhawk 'docky bag', and peregrine survival is undoubtedly helped throughout the year by the large numbers of racing pigeons and feral pigeons available. Consequently natural balances have nothing to do with the problem.

In view of this it makes sense to control magpies, crows and foxes – in fact , it is almost irresponsible not to do so. In its excellent report 'The Silent Fields', on the bird life of Wales, the RSPB admits that nest and chick predation by crows will soon prevent the lapwing from being a breeding bird in most parts of the Principality. Consequently my views on predators and predator control are nothing more than common sense – sadly a commodity that is banned in Suffolk.

By coincidence I was recently filming for Anglia Television's 'Countrywide' programme, in Bradfield Woods – yes owned by the Suffolk Wildlife Trust. And what did I find there? Surprise, surprise, the Suffolk Wildlife Trust is controlling deer. Each year Roe deer, Fallow deer and Muntjac deer are shot. Now I would have thought that according to the Director's logic: 'The numbers of any deer are entirely governed by the vegetation available'. That is the argument used by the anti-elephant cull lobby, that food availabilty will limit the populations of grazers and browsers. So why is the Suffolk Wildlife Trust culling deer? According to their Press Officer 'to protect ash stools and young birch and hazel trees' (a policy that is very sensible and responsible). The message is then, if I understand it correctly: it is conservationally incorrect to kill any creature in order to save a little tern, a roseate tern, a snipe or a song thrush, but it is perfectly alright to kill anything that is damaging a tree stump or eating a flower. How very, very strange. I wonder how the Suffolk Wildlife Trust regards rats?

5

Little Acorns Growing

ક▲

It is now just over a year since the launch of The Countryside Restoration Trust. It has been a momentous year; the response has been both startling and encouraging, and largely due to the generosity of the general public, every aim has been reached. The Trust has purchased its first 22 acres of land; its second block of 18 acres is being bought on Michaelmas Day, September 29th; nearly 900 'Friends of the Countryside' have shown their enthusiasm for the cause and in the last few days the amount of money raised has topped the £100,000 mark. The last £10,000 has arrived with the announcement that the Trust has won first prize in Anglia Water's 'Caring for the Environment Award Scheme, 1994'; there were over 140 entries.

Twelve months ago it was a very different story. Being deeply concerned at the decline in the appearance and wildlife wealth of the general countryside, I had wanted to launch The Countryside Restoration Trust. The aim was to buy intensively farmed land and restore it, not to tell farmers what they should be doing but to show that sympathetic, but profitable, farming can co-exist with wildlife and attractive landscapes, a message that is urgently needed across great swathes of Britain, particularly Eastern England. A landowner had promised us 40 acres of land if we could raise the money, alongside a small tributary of the Cam, but prospects were not good. Indeed a professional fund raiser suggested that if we launched, we would raise only £2000.

The return of otters to the brook forced our hand. We wanted to keep their habitat safe and improve it – we had to go ahead and buy it. After consulting with my fellow Trustees, including Sir Laurens van der Post, Elspeth Huxley, Jane Wallace, Gordon Beningfield, Jonathon Porritt and Jill Barklem, we launched. So unsure was I of the outcome that I literally went cap in hand to friends, relations and trustees trying to secure interest free loans in case the advice of the professional had been correct. Feeling awkward and embarrassed, I begged promises of £20,000. I need not have worried; after my first *Telegraph* article, letters and money flooded in and we bought the first 22 crucial acres, naming it '*Telegraph* Field', after the great surge of cash from readers. The money for the remaining 18 acres, 'Holt Field', is now ready and waiting.

Sadly, the otter holt on the second field no longer appears to be in use. The otters are still very active, leaving regular footprints and 'spraints' (droppings), but badgers appear to have found their wood-pile holt and disturbed them; as a result the otters are now using other resting places in the area, mainly bramble tangles and old willows.

In fact the Trust's stretch of water appears to be one of the busiest otter corridors on the Cam river system. We have not tried to see them for fear of disturbance, but there have been several sightings – unfortunately none made by me. New spraints seem to appear every week. The droppings of mink and otter are best told apart by smell; a mink dropping usually smells of exactly what it is, while an otter dropping has the almost pleasant tang of bloater paste.

In just 12 months the rest of *Telegraph* Field has been transformed from arable monoculture to a rich variety of habitat. The new hedge, nearly 500 yards of it, again planted in the main by *Telegraph* readers in the cold and wet, has been a great success. Almost 99% of the 1800 saplings have survived both their difficult start and the recent drought. Brown hares at one stage decided to try a major pruning job – but we were pleased to see them and most of the chewed young trees have lived. The list of trees and shrubs is impressive; hawthorn, blackthorn, wild privet, field maple, dogwood, wild crab apple, oak, ash, hazel, wild rose, spindle, wild pear and sweet chestnut. We intend to add holly, for the holly blue butterfly, and buckthorn (purging buckthorn and alder buckthorn), the food plants of the caterpillar of the brimstone butterfly.

On one side of the hedge we have planted 8½ acres of Miriam Rothschild's hay meadow mixture. Again, because of the cold, wet spring it had a dreadful start, but when warmer rain came it grew quickly, and despite the current dry, it appears to be doing well. It will take several years to settle down and to suppress the arable weeds, but already clover, bird's foot trefoil and many small grasses are showing that a good start has been made.

On the other side of the new hedge a tenant farmer has just harvested a very good crop of barley, grown with unsprayed headlands. When Dr Dick Potts, Director General of the Game Conservancy, visited the site he was impressed. In the headlands he found insects and plants vital to the survival of young birds and he saw English (grey) partridges, too: 'You know you have a rare bird here', he said excitedly. In fact in half an hour he saw more English partridges on the Trust's few acres than he sometimes sees on complete 10,000 acre estates in a whole day.

In any effort at restoration, co-operation is required. The NRA has been very helpful, digging out an old meander, filled in during 1971, the height of drainage mania. They have tried to raise the water level with two flint riffles containing many tons of flint. With the recent drought the riffles have not been entirely successful as the low flow has allowed the water to flow through the flint, instead of being stopped by it. Perhaps a winter's silt will block the holes; failing this we will consider a plug of clay.

Around the meander we have planted purple loosestrife, marsh marigold, water avens, yellow iris, ragged robin, monkey flower, hemp agrimony, water mint and water forget-me-not. At the moment, the loosestrife, the 'long purples' of John Clare, looks a picture.

But restoration also involves hard work. There has been watering, weeding and topping to undertake, and work is continuing. Already wildlife is returning; the first breeding birds at the meander were a pair of wild mandarin ducks, while one evening I stood and watched a hobby for 20 minutes as it hunted spectacularly over the barley.

The most recent and surprising arrivals were spotted only last week by Robert Goodden, the butterfly expert, who instantly saw several attractive brown argus butterflies feeding on the flowers of bird's foot trefoil. They are beautiful little butterflies and we are lucky to have them. Robert Goodden was pleased by what he saw: 'It is such a good way of showing farmers that conservationists are not against farming practice. It is a tangible example to farmers of good farming with rich wildlife and you are showing how quickly restoration can be done. It is a very important asset to conservation'.

Dr Dick Potts was just as flattering after his visit. 'It was wonderful and quite astonishing to see the bio-diversity brought back in just a year'. Last week the site was visited by Sir Laurens van der Post and he too was impressed by what he saw, and by the way in which the Trust has grown. He said 'I used to think in terms of leaders and that a nation needed leaders, or it couldn't go anywhere and one used to think in conservation that we want to train leaders; but it has gradually dawned on me that this whole concept is out of date. It is no good waiting for leaders, we have to lead ourselves and by forming the CRT you have lead yourselves. You are now leading by what you do, by the example you set, and I find this example of immense, not only local, but of national importance. Everything around that is important starts in a small way'.

Now, with a secretary just employed, and a Director about to be appointed, thanks to generous financial help from the Countryside Commission and the Ernest Cook Trust, we are ready to take our next step, or jump in the dark. We now want to raise over a million pounds to buy, and restore a complete English farm. To do on a large scale, on a prairie farm, what we have done and are still doing on a transformed field. We want barn owls and bee orchids thriving between the crops of cereals and we want livestock grazing in sensibly sized fields, fringed with trees. We want the general countryside to return to being a place of beauty, rich in wildlife, while at the same time producing good food and keeping jobs on the land; we have already seen that it can be done. In a year a small dream has become reality; now we want to extend our vision.

6

Nightmare to Nowhere

ɤ

Life is full of surprises. Suddenly, out of the blue came a call to head south. The BBC wanted me to go to Zimbabwe, at two days notice, to visit some real live peasants. There was not even time to get terrified and neurotic about flying. The intention was to visit peasant farmers near the old Fort Victoria, now called Masvingo. Why they can't use the old names, I have no idea, I suppose it is for the same reason that we say St Albans instead of Verulamium.

The aim of the visit was to see work being carried out by the British-based Intermediate Technology Development Group, designed to encourage peasant farmers to use their 'intermediate technology' – hoes, buckets and women – to the best advantage. It was sensible and much needed work, using ridges along contours to collect rainfall and to stop soil erosion, and the construction of infiltration pits (large holes) to collect water and slow down surface run-off. My African guide, Kuda Muswira, was knowledgeable, enthusiastic and full of hope. But these visits always depress me, for with every advance, Africa's booming population growth means that each step forward is never enough. The stride is always too short. It is chasing an elusive shadow, with the real shadows of hunger, disease and calamity, just around the corner.

African Africa is a humbling experience too – eating a simple dish of millet meal and boiled chicken with your fingers in an

African hut, knowing that the chicken, or, more accurately, the scraggy old hen, has been killed especially for the occasion. It is probably their one and only real meal of the day. I call myself an English peasant, I *am* an English peasant, but I am rolling in money and luxury compared to these toiling, happy, courteous people.

Another aim of Intermediate Technology is to discourage the growing of mono-culture maize and to encourage the use of more drought resistant, indigenous crops, such as sorghum and millet – 'bio-diversity' is the aim, as well as the 'in' word. As I left the area, one thing struck me. All possible land was being used; there were few trees; maize mono-culture was still rampant and there was no room for wildlife. So, despite the distance in miles and cultures, these peasant people and the barley-barons of East Anglia have much in common. The only real difference is that the African mono-culture peasant is poor; the East Anglian mono-culture barley baron is rich, yet they are both going for maximum production regardless of all else.

Many years ago I vowed that I would never again travel on an African bus. Sadly I had to break my own promise. In years gone by I would travel on African buses as part of the 'ethnic experience'; by now I have had my share of ethnic experiences, thankyou very much. Alas, Masvingo's three hire cars were all hired out, leaving me with no other option but to catch an African bus back to Harare. Fortunately, on this occasion, my fellow passengers did not include flapping cockerels and goats, but we were packed on board like sardines. Suddenly, with the bus travelling like a rocket, a large breast and a baby appeared in front of me, neither of which were mine. The vast lady in the next seat had decided to feed her infant, almost giving me concussion as she prepared herself. The man in front also felt hungry; he was eating peanuts and throwing the shells over his shoulder, obviously thinking the baby was ready for solids.

With attack from the front and the side, it was then the turn of the man directly behind me to start coughing, long, throaty coughs, down my neck. For some strange reason my window was the only one open; as a result the atmosphere in the bus turned to steam. All the time the driver drove faster and faster. It was like a roller-coaster ride at the fun fair. I'm sure the large lady next to me was beginning to feed her baby freshly battered butter.

We stopped briefly at a roadside cafe-cum-butchery. Oh Mr Gummer, Mr Waldegrave and MAFF vets, please visit it for your own educations. A man covered with blood was cutting up beef with an electric band-saw and the assorted meat, bone, bone chippings and gristle were being heaped onto the counter, with only brown paper to keep the clouds of flies at bay.

Even more people were crammed in for the final part of the journey. By now I swear the driver had turned into a black Nigel Mansell, complete with moustache. It made flying seem quite safe by comparison. When Nigel Mansell braked suddenly there was no danger that the standing passengers would fall over, they were crammed in too tightly. It reminded me of a story I heard from one young tourist; while travelling in an over-crowded Kenyan bus, he had taken his left foot off the ground to scratch his right foot and then been unable to find a space to put it down again.

At one stop, the in-bus entertainment was two passengers trying to get off at the same time, with neither giving way for the other – perhaps goats were not so bad after all. On the outskirts of Harare, middle class African homes seemed to have metal cages instead of garages for their cars in an attempt to stop theft, while in the township where journey ended, every small house was overflowing with toddlers. The country does not need urgent agricultural 'intermediate technology'; it needs an urgent policy of population control.

Finally the Hell on wheels rolled to a standstill. I staggered out, crushed, jolted and smelling of babies. I swore once more that I would never, ever again travel on an African bus.

7

Painter and Landscape Decorator

ɜ⋑

In a recent newspaper article I mentioned goshawks. It had almost the same effect as any mention of sparrowhawks and magpies. It is clear from many readers that the goshawk is well and truly back. It is thought that following a period of persecution and near extinction, birds were brought over from the continent by falconers and released. With better protection and more forestry plantations these magnificent killing machines have done well. Indeed some people think they have done too well, as they have seen their ornamental doves and pet bantams disappear in a cloud of flying feathers.

One report of a male goshawk was not angry, it was simply a statement of fact. It came from a near neighbour. Will Garfit is a painter – painter, as in artist, not painter and decorator, and he has had a male goshawk fly through the willows around his gravel pits.

When I first knew Will Garfit he looked like a country artist, well dressed and well groomed, in fact almost a country gentleman. How times have changed. Now on occasions he looks almost similar to a down-trodden peasant like me. It is strange how we peasants manage to survive.

He must be one of the few successful artists with callouses of hard skin on his hands and when he is labouring around his beloved gravel pits he looks like an itinerant Irish navvy, not somebody who studied at the Royal Academy. Frequently visitors wanting to fish, or simply to meet the famous artist greet him with 'Can you tell me where the boss is, mate?'.

His gravel pits, his calloused hands and his paintings, particularly those of water, are all part of the same story. In 1969 Will Garfit bought 90 acres of disused gravel pits. They were a wilderness, a dead wilderness, too overgrown and silted up for wildlife. In just 20 years they have been transformed. Open water has appeared; woods have been planted, glades created and nature has come back. There is deep water, shallow water and muddy scrapes. A walk with Will is a revelation; with paths and tracks, among trees, pools and open spaces, the 90 acres seem to double or even treble in size. At every turn he talks enthusiastically about the butterflies here, the rare plants there, 'and you should see the orchids when they are flowering'. At that pool a kingfisher is seen regularly 'and over there a migrating osprey swung under the electric wires, took a large carp, swerved around the wires again and away it went – it was incredible'.

But the whole place is more than just a wildlife reserve, with local naturalists queueing up to carry out various surveys; in some of the pits he breeds crayfish commercially; around the outside he has a successful tree nursery (hence the calloused hands), selling not saplings, but 20-feet-high trees to developers and landscape architects; then there is a carp fishery and a trout fishery, as well as Will's famous shoot, with some of the best shots in the land checking their post every morning, hoping for an invitation.

Once he invited me, a non-shooter, to be a beater. Never again. It was spectacular and I received a brace of pheasants, free-range, organic pheasants, in addition to my pay, but the thorns, hidden holes full of water and the double-backward-somersault into a bramble tangle persuaded me that £250 a day would still not be enough for a second dose. Strangely, he has locals queueing up for that, too; it's amazing what some people will do to avoid the washing-up.

27

So, his 90 acres is a wildlife haven; it makes a profit; it gives his pheasants a free and happy life until they meet the stuffing and the bread sauce, and it inspires one of our best landscape painters. It is astonishing how so many of our great artists, past and present, have also been naturalist/sportsmen. The links between country sports, conservation, sympathetic farming, art and literature are obvious; it is a pity that so many critics of traditional country life seem incapable of seeing them.

Now the links can be seen even more clearly. Holland and Holland, the famous gunmakers, whose guns are slightly too expensive to be used by peasants like me from their bathroom window to frighten magpies, have opened a new gallery at their Bruton Street premises in the Black Hole (London).

Another good artist friend, Gordon Beningfield, also acknowledges the importance of shooting in his early art, as an aid to improving his knowledge of natural history. Now, like me, he is a non-shooter, but like me too he never, ever refuses a pheasant for Sunday dinner. But even now he misses shooting, not so much the pulling of the trigger, but the whole atmosphere of the shoot. 'I miss getting there in the early morning – the smell of dampness and autumn leaves; the gun-dogs eager to work, the chatter and laughter with your friends and then the day – woods, meadows and water – I didn't have to shoot to enjoy it. And finally there was the log fire in the pub at the end of the day, with stories of missed birds; the spaniel chasing the fox, the pheasant falling on the keeper's head – yes, I do miss it'.

Sadly for the shooting world Bramble is no gun-dog. Whenever he hears a shot his tall goes between his legs and he looks worried. The other day he committed the gun dog's cardinal sin; he suddenly dived into a tuft of coarse grass and a tail-less cock pheasant rose skywards, protesting loudly. Bramble had developed a tail at both ends, hair at the rear, feathers at the front. Now that would have made a good painting for Will Garfit's brush.

8

Tree Glee

ɜ⅋

I managed to accomplish something quite remarkable the other day: I planted a tree in the Fens. For all those prairie farmers in East Anglia, and land managers of institutionally owned land, a tree is a green thing with leaves and branches. You probably had a small one in your living room over Christmas, covered with lights. Now imagine something much bigger, growing in the corner of a field, without lights, yes, that's right, a tree: A TREE.

Unfortunately most Fenmen seem to be allergic to trees, and so have managed to turn one of the flattest landscapes in the world, to one of the most artificially treeless. Indeed, a few years ago an old great-uncle of mine, a fine old countryman, moved from the heart of the Fens to where I live now. His first task was to turn the attractive country garden with old trees, shrubs and lawn into a piece of replica Fen. In all other respects he was a wonderful old boy, but like so many others with black fen soil on their boots, and dust blows in their lungs, he simply failed to appreciate trees that could not bear apples or plums.

The garden became a rectangle of maximum fruit and vegetable productlon. What his ancestors had managed to do to the whole of fenland, he did to my present garden. Since I moved in 12 years ago the soil rectangle has reverted; it is now a place for minimum productlon where brambles and planted trees have formed a miniature enclosure.

29

Fenmen defend their fixation on felling and grubbing out by saying: 'There never were any trees in the Fens anyway'. This is rubbish, of course, as old bog oaks are still being uncovered through cultivation, great ancient oaks, pickled in bog. They were not carted to the fens, they grew there.

It is strange how fantasies often repeated become accepted as fact. In his excellent book: *The Illustrated History of the Countryside*, which I recently read again, Dr Oliver Rackham calls the process 'pseudo-history': 'Pseudo-history' is made up of 'factoids'. A factoid looks like a fact, is respected as a fact, and has all the properties of a fact except that it is not true. So, sorry, all those Fenmen who have been saying for years 'There were never any trees in the Fens', you are guilty of passing on pseudo-history, as are those prairie farmers who claim rather amusingly: 'There were never any hedges until the Enclosures'. The pseudo-history and factoids put about by the anti-hunting lobby, and accepted by otherwise normal people would take too long to list here.

My tree was planted with a shiny new spade. It was the first one to be planted in what will grow into a new wood, just outside the Fenland town of March. With help from the Woodland Trust, 16½ acres of land were purchased and 1100 trees have now been planted.

The whole idea for the wood came from the local people. They are naturally conservative, and Conservative, but after 15 years of witnessing governmental conservation trivia, such as the National Forest, which is neither national, nor a forest, they decided that they could wait no longer. They would do something themselves.

Inevitably the local MP attended the planting. Arriving almost last he was not content parking at the end of a long line of cars; he drove up and parked in the field gateway itself, reversing carefully down the slope. As he walked over the plough he commented about the 'heavy land'. Was I hearing right? A rural MP calling fenland soil heavy? If he had tried walking over our fields on the same day his boots would have come off in the mud. As volunteers began planting, he strolled about grandly, before leaving almost as quickly as he had arrived, with hands still clean. He sat in his large car with its 'Westminster' parking sticker displayed prominently, and there he continued to sit – he was stuck. He had done what no true country person would ever do, park downhill in a field gateway in soggy winter. Some peasants duly arrived and pushed this man of the people back onto the road, then, with a smile and wave he was gone. MPs complain of caricatures, cartoons and satire holding them up to ridicule; who needs all that when there is real life?

I have decided that my new year's resolution is to plant more trees. They are the lungs of the planet; by planting trees we are being responsible not only to ourselves but also to future generations. An old country proverb sums it up well:

'He that plants trees loves others besides himself'.

I hope a northern friend of mine has better luck this New Year's Eve than last – no it was not my friend, the wonderful Mr Poole. He drank so much refreshment during the evening that when returning home over a field, in his ATV (all terrain vehicle), he had to stop for a call of nature. He foolishly turned the engine and lights off and was perfectly happy until fully relieved. In the pitch black of a highland night the vehicle had disappeared. He found it again, with the dawn, exactly where he had stopped it.

9

Like a Lamb for the Slaughter

≥▲

There has been much indignation recently concerning the transportation of live farm animals to the continent, and elsewhere, for slaughter. It has been entirely justified as the trade is immoral, inhumane and indefensible. I simply do not understand those of my fellow farmers, often supported unconvincingly by the NFU, who seem to lose interest in their animals once they have left the farm gate and the prospect of a cheque looms.

What has been forgotten in the controversy however, is the fact that thanks to Mr Gummer and the closure of hundreds of slaughterhouses in Britain under his inauspicious reign at the Ministry of Agriculture, even animals slaughtered in this country are frequently being transported great distances, involving journeys over many hours. It is ironic too that dear Mr Gummer saw the closure of so many slaughterhouses, as hundreds of animals are exported simply so that they can be killed and re-imported to Britain as meat. It goes almost without saying that many of the foreign slaughterhouses used are of a lower standard than those forced to close down in Britain. What a way to run a country; what a way to ruin a once thriving business.

Last week it was the turn of my sheep to be sold. I use a good company; the animals went straight for slaughter – missing out a stop at market, and there is no question of them being exported alive. But even so the whole process left me feeling depressed and wondering how much longer I can morally justify keeping livestock. It is hard having morals in an age dominated by market forces, cash flow and 'efficiency'. This government has a lot to answer for.

Just 10 years ago my 26 lambs would have been loaded onto a small lorry and taken to one of several slaughterhouses around Cambridge. The whole process would have been completed comfortably in an hour.

Thanks to Mr Gummer's forced but needless closures, times have changed. Most of the slaughterhouses in the area have closed and so a huge three-tiered animal transporter arrived in the farmyard. My sheep were going to be only part of a load. Via a steep ramp they were driven to the very top of the lorry and several stumbled because of a gap between the top of the ramp and their pen. At least they were not too crowded, or sheared, to cram more on, as is the practice in many parts of the country, even in mid-winter.

After picking up my sheep the driver had several more pick-ups to make, including a number of bullocks the other side of Bedford. My lambs had never been near cattle before, now they would be within feet of them. Then they would be carted beyond Norwich for slaughter. They would experience a meander around the countryside lasting several hours and taking them over 100 miles.

I felt depressed and guilty for the rest of the day. I am not a vegetarian as homo sapiens is a meat-eating species and animal

protein is good for you. But I do not know how much longer I can go on eating and producing meat when the animals I rear humanely and almost naturally have to suffer the stress and trauma of their present Gummerised end. Humanely reared animals, slaughtered quickly, give me no moral qualms; slaughtering after Gummer fills me with dismay. Now, money is put before morality and 'efficiency' before humanity. As a Christian, albeit a bad one, I do not see how Mr Gummer squares the situation created by him, with the values he claims to live by.

Ritual slaughter both at home and abroad is another unsavoury aspect of the current livestock trade. I would never allow one of my animals to go for ritual slaughter. Unfortunately few people speak out against this unacceptable practice for fear of being labelled 'racist', 'fascist', 'anti-semitic' or 'anti-muslim'. I speak out against it simply because it is cruel. A friend who has recently seen ritual slaughter describes it as 'cruel', 'callous' and 'obscene'. He also believes that the standards of hygiene are lower than elsewhere as the Environmental Health Officers fear the 'racism' tag if they complain.

Years ago in hot, dusty climates there were probably sound reasons for ritual slaughter on the grounds of hygiene – to get the blood away from the rest of the carcass. Now, with refrigerators, there is no such need and it is time for this barbaric practice to cease. If any Jews or Muslims feel strongly about their unpleasant and cruel rituals, their solution is clear – they should go and live in a non-Christian country where their own values predominate.

Fortunately I am not the only farmer outraged by the present situation. Talking with a group of farmers recently they all, without exception, claimed that they would not be voting Tory at the next election because of the slaughterhouse issue. It is a sad reflection on the present out of touch Tory hierarchy that it has managed to separate itself from its own grass roots so expertly.

When a tractor breaks down on a big farm, the farmer (or more accurately, the land manager), simply uses one of his others. When a tractor on a small farm breaks down, the farmer is stuck, it is the only one he owns. During the middle of summer our one and only large tractor broke down and we were unable to beg, borrow or steal an immediate replacement. It was at thistle-topping time on our Countryside Stewardship fields where weedkillers are not allowed. As a result our healthy crop of thistles went unmown. At the time I was frustrated, now I am pleased; with the thistle-down has come goldfinches, not one or two but hundreds, family parties and large flocks. Not a single 'charm', but 'charm' after 'charm'. I hope the tractor breaks down again next year.

10

Man's Best Friend

❧

The relationship between Man and Dog goes back thousands of years, almost certainly to Neolithic times. Dogs were around the fires of hunter-gatherers and down through history they remained. As hunting changed to herding they were there; the Romans had them, so did the Normans and the Saxons and they are still very much around today.

Dogs have been used for defence against wild animals, for hunting, herding, security and simply as companions. The relationship has been of great mutual benefit. The dog has secured warmth and food; Man has obtained a willing worker who gives enthusiasm, loyalty and affection.

In Britain today the dog is still working: guarding, guiding, hunting, herding, retrieving, listening and sniffing. Millions of dogs are also doing next to nothing, they are just pampered pets, friends and companions.

I like dogs and have always had them. My present hound, Bramble, is a traditional gypsy running dog, a cross between a whippet and a Bedlington terrier. The mixture of genes was arranged by a tremendous old countryman, Monty Christopher, the retired headkeeper at Sandringham. He wanted to produce a lurcher that looked like a miniature deerhound; with Bramble he succeeded perfectly.

Bramble's function in life is to be a friend and an early warning barking machine, but I like dogs that work for their livings, too. I do not hunt, shoot or fish, but as a rural peasant, irritated by political correctness, I enjoy many aspects of my rural heritage that townies do not seem to understand. Consequently, it gives me pleasure to watch a labrador retrieve a pheasant, foxhounds working a wood and a cattle dog rounding up bullocks in a sea of mud and flying hooves.

Sheepdogs, Border Collies, are a joy, too. We have had several on our small farm and they have all lived as part of the family. I have watched shepherds herding their sheep with dogs all over the country and the bond between man and dog, dog and man is clear to see. It is real, special and moving. Whenever I see this link I am always reminded of those lines by W. H. Davies:

Still do I claim no man can reach
His highest soul's perfection,
Until his life from day to day,
Deserves a dog's affection.

Over the years the dog really has become 'Man's best friend' and Bramble has a special place in my life. Of course, in the cynical, plastic and shallow world in which we live there will be people who sneer and claim that I am suffering from acute sentimentality. That does not worry me in the slightest. There is a place for sentimentality in the lives of most normal people and there are 5.4 million dog owning households in this country, with 7 million dogs, who would agree with me.

But although the dog is usually thought of as a friend, it is becoming increasingly clear that some of the friendship is only one way. Sadly cases of cruelty, indifference and neglect seem to be on the increase. Man's best friend is not getting the treatment he deserves.

This Christmas thousands of puppies will be given as presents. Yet later on when the cuddly little dogs become large noisy dogs , many will be abandoned. Each year dogs are dumped by motorways and in the countryside, when the fun and novelty of dog ownership wear off. Many of these dogs end their lives in pain and misery; hit by a lorry or put down because nobody wants an abandoned, ill-kept stray.

Hundreds of thousands of dogs get killed on our roads annually. Again the dogs are often innocent victims; their deaths are caused by speeding macho-motorists driving like lunatics through towns and villages they do not know and areas they do not understand. To them car ownership and speed are 'rights'; in reality, car ownership is a privilege, and all privileges should carry 'responsibilities'. It is strange how all types and classes of car driver seem to have a complete character change as soon as they start up their car, a trail of dead and damaged dogs is just one of the results of their selfish brand of lunacy.

Large dogs in small houses is another cruelty: a deerhound in a London penthouse flat, never able to run, is simply a piece of executive, living furniture. Indeed that is the fate too of many dogs that are bred for showing; they cease to be dogs, they become things. Often they are almost caricature dogs, in-bred and over-manicured.

Other dogs can simply be chained up all day and left. Alsatian 'guard dogs' in seedy yards with no proper bedding and shelter and border collies, shut up in urban tower-blocks, miles from the open country. That is the ultimate cruelty, a dog bred for work and activity kept shut in an urban prison.

The Government has been cruel, too. Its Dangerous Dogs Act has led to the destruction of many quite harmless dogs, even pit bull terriers. It was never the breed that was unacceptable, only owners who turned their dogs into canine yobs. Similarly many dogs that have attacked children have been wrongfully blamed;

the guilty have been the parents who have allowed small children to crawl all over the dog, pulling its hair, poking its eyes and threatening its food; the wonder is that even more children do not get bitten each year thanks to the stupidity of their parents.

The Government's cruelty spreads as well to its anti-rabies legislation. Rabies is a terrible disease and it should be kept out of Britain; but it has been here before and it is easy to control without the widespread destruction of wildlife and dogs planned by the government. In Africa, France, or wherever, the solution is simple – the infected animal is quickly shot and people who have been near it are inoculated.

Under government rules all dogs coming into Britain have to be put into quarantine for six months, causing anguish for dogs and owners alike. Friends of mine returning from Africa with their dogs were so upset by this prospect that they, and their animals, now live happily in France. All they needed, and had, for the French were current inoculation certificates. It is astonishing; horses can catch and carry rabies, yet they are allowed to move across the world to compete in equestrian events, yet a champion sheepdog is not allowed to compete in Europe or America without facing quarantine. It is inconsistent, unfair and without reason. Yet there is now tried and tested anti rabies vaccine available – used by all and sundry – except the British. The sooner inoculatlon replaces isolation the better for dogs and owners. It would also mean that I could take Bramble to meet my friends marooned in France.

Unfortunately dogs face yet another worrying and increasing threat. More and more dogs, 23% of them, are now dying from cancer. It is a growing and heart-rending problem. Pesticides, pollutants, vaccines or even veterinary medicines could be contributary factors, as could too little exercise and too much food.

The British have a reputation for being a nation of animal lovers; in the case of dogs, I wish it was still deserved.

11

One Man and His Fleas

ða

So, my first series of 'One Man and His Dog' has been seen on the telly. It was a wonderful series to film; the setting at Buttermere was perfect; the shepherds, sheep dogs and the Herdwick sheep were a pleasure to meet and the BBC crew could not have been more pleasant. I have met television people before, some of whom have been so weighed down by the size of their egoes and medallions that they were living caricatures of pomposity. Yet without exception the crew at Buttermere were helpful, skilful and above all humourous. Without them Bramble, me and commentator Gus Dermody would not have got through.

It is a nerve-racking experience looking into a television camera, with no interviewer to talk to. I knew that out there, beyond the lense, there would be thousands of viewers going: 'Isn't he fat', 'short', 'ugly' and 'when are they going to bring Phil Drabble back out of retirement'.

Then, nearer to home, there would be my friends. I was right to worry, for now, whenever I go into my local pub I am greeted with a cacophony of bleating sheep and cries of 'Come by'. I don't know what is being put into their drinks. Their television reactions have been identical: raucous laughter followed by 'I didn't know he had a tie', 'Where did he get that jacket?', 'Why don't they stand him on a box?' and 'has he had elocution lessons?'.

The professional television critics have also had their fun. The *Telegraph's* own unfortunately named Stephen Pile described me as looking like a Toby Jug. The *Evening Standard* referred to Gus and myself as 'a couple of middle-aged male models selling thermal underwear'. That was amazingly accurate, for when I was offered the job I suddenly realised that I had no clothes, including decent long-johns. All I had was one suit for births, marriages and deaths and a collection of jeans, jumpers, wellies and a scruffy Barbour jacket that had been through too many bramble bushes, over too many muck heaps and to the top of Mount Kilimanjaro. So what should I do? Off-the-peg clothes have more chance of fitting Bramble than me.

Fortunately Gordon Beningfield came to the rescue by mentioning John Brocklehurst, 'The Countryman's Outfitter' from Bakewell. It was a good choice because John Brocklehurst is a fine, down-to-earth countryman with a sense of humour – he needed it, to fit somebody my shape. He started his business

selling wellies and buckets to farmers from the back of a van. Now he manufactures his own line of clothing and his van has grown to a huge lorry that visits a host of country shows and fairs. He says that off-the-peg clothes never fit country people who do physical work. We are apparently too broad and thick, 'thick' as in body thickness, I hasten to say. The final bill came to – well, a lot, as I had nothing. Now I have enough smart clothes to last me a lifetime, wearing them once a year for as long as 'One Man and His Dog' continues.

I have had many kind letters about my little dog Bramble, including one from Swaffham, in Norfolk, sent by the lovely lady, Margaret Wilson, who owned his mother. She has reprimanded me for calling Bramble a cross between a whippet and Bedlington terrier. His mother was apparently not a whippet but a Norfolk lurcher. It was a mistake on my part, but of course to anybody from the Swaffham area, calling a lurcher a whippet is almost a capital offence.

Many of the letters claimed that the series did not show enough of Bramble. I suppose the BBC limited his appearances in case he became a cult figure and demanded higher wages – prime cut beef, or even pheasant, instead of Bonios.

Fame has not gone to Bramble's head, but something else has. For weeks he has been absolutely lousy. He has been covered with big fleas, little fleas, brown fleas and black fleas. They all have three things in common – they jump huge distances, they bite and they seem to thrive on flea powder. I have sprinkled him, sprayed him and washed him, all with the same result, the fleas have remained happy and highly active.

Visitors who attempt to sit on my settee have been given a formal flea warning and a financial disclaimer, yet they still take the plunge. My pretty little cousin ignored my warning shortly before her wedding. She paid the price in full and as I understand it, she was so covered in bright red spots on the palest parts of her body, that she had to lock the bedroom door and hide the key to prevent her new husband from taking flight and rushing back to Wales on their wedding night.

My vet has never known a flea year like it. In desperation, and against my better judgement, I listened to him and used an organophosphorous drip to get rid of our little black, jumping friends. It appears to have worked and the fleas have gone. But something attacked me at the same time. As the smell of OP flea killer drifted through the house I developed flu-like symptoms. I suddenly had a headache, a sore throat and my asthma came back. I think I should have stuck with the fleas.

While at my favourite cousin's wedding I once again managed to show the depth and quality of my upbringing. As a waitress walked by I asked her if she would get the mayonnaise from the middle of the table. She was not impressed: 'That is not mayonnaise, sir. It's the sour cream you should have eaten with your soup' – so there! I hope that one day I have the pleasure of asking her to sit down on my settee.

12

Food for Thought

ะ๑

This is a difficult time of the year for me. It is the season of the lunch, dinner and supper. Will I speak here? Will I speak there? And, for the sake of the Countryside Restoration Trust, I almost always say 'Yes'. Unfortunately that is not the end of the story, for at every function I get asked other questions – would I like a starter, steak and kidney pie, turkey, beef, profiteroles, sherry trifle or spotted dick? Sadly, I always say yes to these questions, too. I simply love traditional food, healthy or unhealthy; I like it all. Well, almost: I draw the line at treacle tart, ginger cake and bread and butter pudding.

Consequently I have put on nearly a stone in a month and there is still nearly another month to go before Christmas. I am beginning to make the diabolical Mr Blobby look distinctly anorexic. Normally at this time of year I have one excellent way of fighting the battle of the bulge: splitting logs. Now, just when I want the exercise, the weather has been so mild that there has been no need for fires and the axe remains unused.

One function I enjoyed attending recently was the Twenty-Fifth Anniversary Conference of the Cornwall Farming and Wildlife Advisory Group (FWAG). The Pavilion at the Royal Cornwall Showground at Wadebridge was packed, not with dignitaries and professional conservationists, but mainly with working farmers, most of them running small farms. The car park told a significant story: it was full of practical cars and pick-ups – these were farmers who had mud on their boots, and in their cars, and who were interested in conservation, too. Not only were they interested in conservation, many of them prac-tised it as part of their normal farming husbandry, for on many traditional Cornish farms there are still orchids, wet areas, barn owls and otters. Small farms, traditional farms and people work-ing close to the land create a sympathy for wildlife and a desire to know more, hence the packed hall.

On the same day, Cambridgeshire FWAG also held an event for FWAG's 25th birthday. It has an excellent county officer, John Terry, whose post is funded by Ciba Geigy. He is knowl-edgeable, amiable and helpful. At that event only about ten actual farmers attended and like nearly all farming functions in Cambridgeshire, the car park resembled a beauty contest for Range Rovers, spotless on the outside, as well as on the inside.

So the county which desperately needs conservation on its rolling, treeless acres, showed virtually no interest in PWAG's anniversary. While the county that already has numerous ex-amples of farming and conservation, Cornwall, was full of inter-est and enthusiasm.

The comparison between Cornwall and Cambridgeshire was interesting for another, deeper reason. Many of the smaller farms in Cornwall are currently going through a cash-flow crisis, yet they carry on their conservation-friendly farming with little direct help from the great EU. The largely indifferent Cambridgeshire farmers however, are awash with money, thanks to the largesse of the EU and the British taxpayer. So those large farmers interested only in efficiency, profit margins and money are receiving great pocketfuls of the stuff. While those small farmers practising conservation and who help, can whistle in the wind.

The only strange note at the Cornwall Conference was struck by one of FWAG's national chairmen. As a large Wiltshire farmer, farming some 3000 acres, he mentioned how he had been pleasantly surprised by the GAP reforms, although it was 'inevitable' that many small farmers would go out of business. What he failed to say was that the reason they would be going out of business was that the money they needed was going to the big boys like him – so of course he would like CAP reform, wouldn't he? Any day now farmers with vast arable acres, even those whose fields are wildlife dead, will be receiving anything up to £100,000 per 1000 acres as their yearly CAP reform payments (IACS payments – the Integrated Area Compensatory Scheme payments will amount to hundreds of millions of pounds this year); while the small farmer running a traditional mixed farm of 100 acres, with skylarks and orchids, may be struggling to collect £2000. It is hardly surprising therefore that small farms will be 'inevitably' lost.

A neighbouring farmer, with a large farm, believes that if this Euro nonsense continues then in a few years time the farms of Eastern England will have grown to one per parish, affecting the village shop, the village school, the church and the pub. Why the government did not put an acreage limit on CAP money, of say 600 acres, or make all payments conditional on a means test, schemes for creating rural employment and for improving wildlife habitats is almost beyond belief. The money currently being poured into the pockets of those who do not really need it should have been used to keep people on the land and to help rural communities, not to destroy jobs and family farms to the detriment of village life. One large East Anglian farmer who will be receiving a six-figure cheque any day has been quite honest with me: 'We've had a good year and don't really need it – but if you were in my position would you send the cheque back?'. Why the tabloid press has not got on to this scandal is a mystery; I suppose they don't understand it.

My local agricultural engineer is feeling the effects of the current fiasco. After building up his successful small repair service from nothing, he now has virtually no work and has just laid off one of his workers. He is fuming: 'The farmers are getting so much money that they are all buying huge, new and expensive equipment. There is nothing to go wrong, it's madness'. It is, and we are all paying for it.

13

Moon Shadows

❧

I suppose that I am a bit of a throwback, as I find it almost impossible to sleep with the curtains closed. In fact the only time I try is when I have the misfortune to be staying in a city. Then, closing the curtains is the only way of shutting out the never ending urban lights of the night and the noise.

My mind and body like the dark, it gives rest, peace, and, believe it or not, illumination. From my bed I look straight out into the night sky; stars, the moon or cloud-filled darkness, I like them all. I am baffled how modern man seems so fearful of the dark. From the Bushman of Southern Africa, to the Aborigines of Australia and the Red Indians of North America, the night sky was, and is, part map, part story and part mystery.

From my bedroom window I still experience all three. I see those stars, planets and constellations mapped out in their constantly moving display, the Plough, Orion's Belt and the Milky Way. Sometimes I lie and wonder at their clarity and immensity; feelings that have been felt by ploughmen, shepherds and men at sea for many generations.

On a clear night when I see a fox walking stealthily through my garden I intrude on an unfinished story. Its graceful body casts a moon-shadow at this time of year and even in the darkness its breath is the colour of frost:

He passes into darkness
As cloud restores the night;
A pheasant calls in warning, of footsteps that bring fear;
The air sighs.
Beneath the trees a shadow hunts,
Time freezes and a rabbit dies;
A dog barks as moonlight falls on blood-stained grass.
The fox has gone.

Owls do not need the moon and they are active close to my house even on the darkest night. They provide mystery. What are they doing? How are they hunting? What do they see? There are tawnys who, with daylight, have vanished, roosting in a tree-hole or close to an ivy-covered trunk. Little owls also disappear with the dawn, although they can sometimes be seen during daylight peering comically and inquisitively from behind a branch. It is my dream that one day before my longest night, I will also see barn owls hunting the fields beyond my garden.

At this time too there are other mysteries in the night. Travellers passing overhead and through the darkness. Only occasionally do I see a fast, fleeting shadow of waders moving north. What are they? Where are they? Why do they travel at night? In the autumn the movement is southwards; in the spring the current of flight is reversed. From the occasional plaintive calls there have been curlews, greenshank and sandpipers. I wonder at their confidence as well as at their navigation.

Enjoying darkness and the sleep it brings has one disadvantage. I wake with the dawn, like any wild bird or beast. In summer I will roll over again and doze, but it means that the nights are short. That is another reason why I like the winter as it means that both the night, and sleep are long.

In the passing of the year I like the way in which we change the time, giving an extra hour in bed from autumn onwards, and getting us out of bed an hour earlier in the spring. This strange system was introduced years ago entirely for the benefit of the farming community, in an age when most of the rural population lived and worked on the land. They could understand the reasons and agreed with them.

During the winter an hour of daylight to the farmer is worth two at dusk. It is a time to check animals, calves, piglets and in late winter, lambs. A midwife, even on a farm, welcomes the light. It is morning light too that is so convenient when fighting the effects of a night of frost. It is easier in daylight to thaw pipes and break ice. February is the month when 'As the days lengthen, so the frosts strengthen'. It is that hour after dawn that is often the coldest and the farmer needs to be there then, not an hour before.

The extra hour in the morning was an arrangement for summer. To make the days longer for hay cart and harvest. Again it was sensible, at a time when people realised the importance of the seasons and the need to fill barns. Now predominantly urban Britain wants to change the time, to join with the rest of Europe and have Central European Time.

It is madness of course as we are not in Central Europe; we have fallen off the Western Edge of Europe, into the Atlantic, and so our geographical and solar time zone cannot be the same as Paris, Geneva and Budapest. Our time is British Time, Greenwich Mean Time. One time zone for the whole of Europe would be like telling the East Coast of the United States that it must have the same time as the West. I don't think the Americans would be pleased.

If these sad urbanites, so out of touch with their own seasons and time zones, desperately want to phone, fax or just copy the ways of the rest of Europe, the solution is simple. They should work from 8 am to 4 pm instead of from 9 to 5. Failing this they could always go to live on mainland Europe. So I say to the great urban majority: 'Please leave my time alone. I like it as it is; it's British, and so am I'.

14

Rudolph and Fred

❧

It is that time of year again, when customers flock to the farm in droves, not to buy free-range eggs, turkeys or even the odd goose, but to see Father Christmas. We have become one of the few farms in the country, not only to receive a visit from the great man himself, but we also give bed and breakfast to his reindeer. In return he gives the admission money to the Countryside Restoration Trust; he really is a generous man.

This year, fortunately, Father Christmas managed to keep his trousers aloft for the duration of his visit and despite a marginal late arrival, due to heavy traffic on the M25, the visit almost went perfectly. Surprisingly none of the gathering asked why Father Christmas needed a free-flow of traffic on the M25 when he could have simply put his reindeer into gear and flown to the farm.

Apparently the answer to the puzzle is quite simple. Father Christmas can only get his beasts to fly after sprinkling them with star-dust. This substance, not subsidised by the EU, or banned – yet – by a Brussels Directive, is so expensive that Santa can only afford to use it on Christmas Eve. That seems a reasonable explanation to me. Perhaps that is why the Chancellor wanted to put VAT on fuel, so that the Government could afford to buy some of this precious stuff. Sprinkled liberally over the Cabinet it could at last give them a bit of colour and sparkle.

We only had one dissatisfied customer this year, a little boy from Royston. He wanted to see Rudolph, complete with red nose. Sadly, on that day Rudolph was tired and not available for public acclaim; he was resting up for his big day. The other thing of course, is that a reindeer's nose only glows red when it is flying at high altitude and shortly after landing. A reindeer actually has a hair-covered nose, unlike almost all other mammals. Consequently this winter, temperatures have been so warm that Rudolph has simply not been able to get his nose to glow. Poor Toby from Royston was not simply upset, he was distraught; his whole life had revolved around meeting Rudolph.

Fortunately his wish will soon be granted; next time the reindeer visit the farm he will see Rudolph. Gustav, the bull with magnificent antlers, is to change his name briefly, by deed poll.

The reindeer are part of the Cairngorm herd, owned by the remarkable Alan and Tilly Smith. Their promotional winter visits to shopping centres and film studios make the herd financially viable without having to resort to the the butcher's knife and tastefully produced Rudolph-burgers. With just a few animals in the lorry, movement is simple and stress free and shows that animals can be transported humanely in smallish lorries, with few passengers.

Almost inevitably I had a stupid question from a newspaper reporter this year: 'Isn't it demeaning for the reindeer to be carted about so that people can stare at them all day?'. The excited eyes of numerous children and the relaxed state of the reindeer give their own answer. In any case reindeer have lived in semi-domestication for hundreds of years, and their long association with Man is shown in their laid-back reaction to people and fairy lights. My answer to the reporter was simple: 'If the reindeer were not working for Father Christmas, the herd would have to pay for itself in other ways. Would you prefer them to be killed and eaten, as in Lapland, and do you find reindeer burgers more attractive than Father Christmas and tradition?' Political correctness was overcome and suddenly tradition and Father Christmas became acceptable.

I love the build-up to Christmas, the traditional story, carols, decorations, sloe gin, the lot. I also like seasonal verses, however good or bad. It always amazes me that each year I get several requests for copies of a poem I quoted in *The Daily Telegraph* 15 or 16 years ago. People still remember it and write complaining that they have lost their cut-out copy and want to quote it on Christmas cards or read it at a carol service. It was written by an ordinary farmworker in my village, Charlie Disbrey. He was a fine simple man, with simple tastes, who loved the countryside and had a way with words. In a different world, or a more educated world, he could easily have been a writer or a poet, but his talents had no outlet and like many men of his generation he accepted his lot and because of it, the farm on which he worked was a better place. He died a few years ago, but his Christmas poem, 'The Story of Donkey Fred' lives on, inspired by a donkey on the bridleway to Grantchester. Sadly the donkey has also gone. I hope readers old and new enjoy his simple poem:

Old Fred he stands with downcast eye,
He shakes his head and wonders why,
This empty meadow for my home
And I stand sadly here alone.

He calls to mind a summer day
And folk who walked the Bridleway,
Who stayed awhile and had a chat
And gave old Fred a friendly pat.

He wonders if it's true, that when,
A donkey went to Bethlehem,
That Mary on his back did ride
With Joseph walking at her side.

And now the stars are shining bright
And darkness falls, once more 'tis night,
Now all is quiet, and donkey Fred
Walks slowly to his humble shed.

And underneath the starlit beams
Old Fred the donkey sleeps and dreams,
With shepherds poor and the wise men
He walks the road to Bethlehem.

And one bright star looked down and led
Old donkey Fred to Jesu's bed.
He lowly kneels and with a bray
Greets Jesus Christ on Christmas Day.

And Mary said we thank you Fred
For coming to our manger bed,
Tell folk who walk the Bridleway,
You came to us on Christmas Day.

15

Skating on Thin Ice

❧

The New Year started in exactly the way every new year should begin: I was skating. After just three nights of good frost the ice cracked, but even after all the Christmas turkey it could take my weight. It was wonderful to be gliding, without effort, across good ice on a beautiful crisp, clear morning. Skating outside, on natural ice, using speed skates, must be one of the most pleasurable activities ever invented by man. The field at Earith, in the Fens, was half-flooded and with the whole countryside white with ice and frost the setting was perfect. With a chattering

gaggle of geese flying overhead there was no other place in the world I would rather have been and no other activity, or offer, that could have lured me away.

The only surprise was the fact that there were only three of us skating. An old fen codger, who appears with the ice year after year, was skating easily and rhythmically, hands behind his back – he can, and does skate all day. His friend, slightly more professional, was there hoping for long term ice and racing, and then there was me. Ice is the only substance that allows me to move with speed and grace.

Despite the ice, the roads were full of cars, their occupants going to sales and car boot sales – but only three people skating? Thirty years ago there would have been 300 skating. It was another sad sign of the steady urbanisation of Britain, the urbanisation of the mind as well as the body.

The urbanisation of the BBC's weather-forecast happened years ago. Again this year the townee weathermen and women were warning about the 'terrible winter weather' and they could not contain their glee at the thaw. I wish they would remember that some of us actually like true winter and hate the thaw.

The New Year has started with more good news. Several months ago the National Rivers Authority hinted that it planned to turn my little local brook back into an 'efficient drainage channel'. The tone of the NRA's engineering arm was made worse by the fact that its conservation arm had recently been most helpful in making the brook less efficient. So the proposed work would undo all the good work.

The NRA drainage letter which appeared on my doorstep, out of the blue, was insensitive and unwelcome and as Chairman of the Countryside Restoration Trust I wrote indignant letters to the lovely Mr Gummer, Mr Waldegrave, Uncle Tom Cobley and all. The one person I forgot to include on my letter list was the Chairman of the NRA itself, Lord Crickhowell. Instead, he has now written to me a most encouraging letter, a letter that will not only benefit the CRT, but all landowners and farmers interested in conservation. He writes:

This letter [The NRA's frightening letter demanding access and drainage rights], which has been in use for some time, does clearly need to be amended to reflect present day conservation guidelines whilst carrying out flood defence maintenance dredging work, and to be more customer friendly. We will also ensure in future that area flood defence and conservation staff prepare their initial proposals for all maintenance dredging works in advance of letters of notice being forwarded to owner occupiers, and that owners of land with designated sites of conservation interest adjoining main rivers should be consulted prior to the issue of the formal letter.

This change of attitude is a tremendous step forward and I, and the CRT, are grateful to Lord Crickhowell for being so prompt and open. We have now walked our length of brook with officers from the NRA and the work will not only be kept to a minimum, but some positive conservation measures will also be carried out. On two meanders the inside bank will be lowered to create small areas of not simply 'wetland', but really wet land. We hope this will be good for birds such as snipe and lapwing and also become a rich breeding ground for insects.

Although pleased and pleasantly surprised by the NRA's attitude, I have to confess that I still cannot really understand why any work has to be done on this small tributary of the Cam, or for that matter any small tributaries of major rivers. What river engineers have accomplished over the years is simply to move upstream flood waters, downstream. They have lowered water tables and stream bed levels, flushing surface water from the land. This means that after heavy rainfall the floods do not take place on harmless water meadows, but in the lower reaches, where housing development is more likely to occur, such as at York, Chichester and Dundee. This is clever stuff, turning natural, harmless floods into local, dangerous and costly disasters. Perhaps river engineers should be renamed 'flood-movement officers', or even 'flood creation officers'.

I have to confess that the New Year has not been entirely wonderful. While putting on my skates I managed to sit on one of my best winter friends, my attractive *Field* hip-flask. I had put it in my back trouser pocket turning it into a posterior-flask; it was flattened. Later, when I took the cap off for some inner warmth, the sloe-gin squirted out like a miniature fountain. It was not wasted however, as Bramble licked it off the ice. I have always believed sloe gin to be a remarkable drink and for the rest of the day I swear Bramble's tail wagged up and down instead of side to side.

16

The Booty of Language

਒੍ਨ

I have just had to make an escape: an escape from the telephone, knocks on the door and the great bundles of letters that seem to drop into my letter box every day. Simply to run a furrow with a pen across an open page I fled to the Norfolk village of Stiffkey for a week, to a small flint hovel without a phone, to get some time to write.

There, the distractions are different, and more acceptable. Almost devoid of tourists, the North Norfolk coast in winter is how the British countryside ought to be; traditional and quiet, with wildlife everywhere.

Because of the water meadows, salt marshes and acres of foreshore, there is a long tradition of wildfowling in the area. Some of those who brave the cold, mud and treacherous tides have accents so broad that they make Bernard Matthews sound as if he's had elecution lessons.

The thousands of wintering geese really are 'bootifull'. I can think of few more moving sights than the gangs of whiffling geese flying over wild land and sea at dusk and dawn. One afternoon thousands of geese were feeding on a large field of winter wheat. 'What sort are they?' I asked one local farmer who looked as if he would know everything there is to know about Norfolk. 'They're "Been" geese,' he said with feeling. 'They've Been here; they've Been there; they've Been every bloody where.

59

I wish they'd go somewhere else'. In fact they were not Bean geese, they were Pink-Footed and Brent. Normally they do little damage to cereal crops, simply grazing them, as sheep did years ago, and leaving little piles of natural manure in return. However, in wet winters such as this one they can 'puddle' the wheat into the mud causing some losses.

It was good to see water meadows opposite the flint hovel living up to their name. Several were flooded, with the land-owner apparently trying to keep the water on his fields. His rewards were 'packs' of wigeon and several 'springs' of teal, as well as redshank, dunlin, oystercatchers and more moorhens than I have seen for years. I was pleased to see the moorhens, as it showed one thing clearly – an absence of mink. When mink reached our farm and local brook, the moorhens were the first to go, the aperitif before the water voles, kingfishers and mallards. Again the old farmer had words of wisdom to give when I described the problem: 'Aperitif? Is that what you call it? I always thought it was French for a set of dentures'.

The reason for the lack of mink in that part of the country is simple. There are still many shooting estates in the area and the gamekeepers keep the mink at bay. Not only does this benefit pheasants and partridges but it helps wildlife, too, particularly those thousands of ground-nesting birds that journey to the North Norfolk coast to breed every summer.

The farm with the water meadows was said to have been once owned by Henry Williamson, from where he wrote his famous *Story of a Norfolk Farm*. It is also where he discovered that it is almost impossible to farm and write. When you should be writing you are wanted on the farm, and when you want to farm, an editor or a publisher nags you for copy.

I was interested to see the land once worked by the man whose wildlife stories first induced me to read for pleasure. Recently I read *Tarka the Otter* for about the tenth time. It still grips me from first page to last and each time I get to the death of Tarka I have to fight back tears. It remains a mystery to me why Henry Williamson was never honoured for his writing. I wonder what Lord Archer of Weston-super-Mare has got that Henry Williamson hadn't?

The other famous resident of Stiffkey, according to my old father, was the vicar who graced the pulpit between the wars. It was apparently his self-made mission to help rescue 'fallen women'. In his enthusiasm he rescued hundreds – most of them being young and pretty. For his efforts he was un-frocked and later, he could often be seen at Blackpool, during the holiday season, protesting his pure motives from inside a barrel. Later, to emphasise his innocence still further, he would put his head into a lion's mouth, as a test of truthfulness and righteousness. The performance finished at Skegness in spectacular fashion, when the lion too, suddenly thought that it had learnt the true meaning of the word aperitif.

Perhaps the Skegness lion ought to have visited the Red Lion at Stiffkey for a proper starter – parsnip soup. On a cold day I had no idea that parsnips could be transformed into such a delicious food. Parsnip soup, fish pie, Norfolk dumplings, Wherry beer and Abbot Ale. East Anglia in winter certainly has a lot going for it.

Not too far away from Stiffkey a small village has copied some of its larger neighbours and is twinned with a village in France. At a fraternal visit across the Channel last year the dignitaries from the edge of the Fens were trying to make polite conversation during a buffet/reception. They spoke very slowly and loudly to help their Euro-friends comprehend. Complete understanding was reached when the Chairman of the visiting Parish Council picked up a tasty morsel from a plate and said to his opposite number, even more slowly and loudly than usual: 'In England we call this a "vol-au-vent", what do you call it?'.

17

Once More Into the Hedge

৵

What is happening to the weather? Normally Badger Walker arrives on the edge of spring for a day's hedgelaying. To mark the arrival of both the season and the man, the weather usually resembles mid-winter, with ice in the wind and the rain only just liquid. This year, as Badger arrived in the winter, the weather was spring-like; a fact noted by the rooks as they wheeled and tumbled above.

Nothing else had changed, however. Gordon Beningfield arrived to paint the great hedge-layer in action and Will Garfit also rolled up, without his paint brushes, for an audience with the authentic voice of eccentric Britain. This meant that coffee lasted until mid-day.

By the time 'dinner' arrived, half-an-hour later, Badger had just taken his axes and slashers out of his car. Dinner at the farmhouse was another long drawn-out affair: jugged hare preceded by 'light pudding' and gravy that was almost a meal in its own right. Why is it that only my mother's generation seem capable of making gravy worthy of the name? If there was a World Championship in gravy-making, my old mother would win it easily. However, now on her second pacemaker and a cocktail of pills, I am not sure she would get through the drugs test.

Jugged hare, with carrots floating in the gravy, stuffing balls and red-currant jelly, washed down with elderflower wine is definitely the meal for winter. I can think of only one better, roast pheasant. l am really pleased that vegetarianism is on the increase in this country – it means more hare and pheasant for me, thank you very much.

It also saves me from the guilt that many vegetarians conveniently choose to ignore. That guilt should result from the indigenous forests felled in South America to enable soya beans to be grown. Sadly the moral sensibilities of affluent vegetarians often do not venture beyond their own dinner plates. Whatever the diet, there is a moral dilemma at every turn. I happen to prefer free-range, humanely killed protein to expensive vegetable protein grown on land taken from flattened forests.

We staggered out of the farmhouse at 2.30, wanting a snooze rather than a hedge. I dared not even think of my armchair; that would have meant the whole afternoon disappearing, too. On reaching the hedge Badger worked with a sudden burst of energy, sawing, slashing and laying with great enthusiasm. He was in danger of destroying a relaxed tradition. Fortunately I soon managed to slow him down. As he slashed away, I heaped up the trimmings into a large bonfire, up wind, instead of down. Green hawthorn hedge trimmings send out clouds of smoke before they become hot enough to really burn. Soon Badger disappeared in a wall of thick, choking smoke. He emerged wheezing and coughing: 'You daft. . . . What did you do that for?'

'I thought you wanted a rest'.

As the smoke proceeded to hide the hedge Badger made a remarkable confession. On Boxing Day, as a surprise present, he had decided to take his friend Daisy to Prague, to Wenceslas Square, for the day – how romantic. It was such a surprise to Daisy, that on arrival at the airport she discovered that her passport had just expired. Being the perfect gentleman, Badger packed her off home and went to Wenceslas Square alone. Who said the age of romance and chivalry was dead?

Being in a confessing mood Badger also told the tale of his first communion at his local church. He was so nervous when the chalice full of wine arrived that he was not sure how much he was supposed to drink. The vicar soon told him: 'Steady up lad, you're not at the Nag's Head now'.

Flame caught hold; heat drove the smoke away and Badger was able to resume. Last year I was convinced that it was impossible to do less work in a day; I was wrong – this year it was almost a waste of time starting. At the end of the day we felt so guilty that Badger decided to come back for another day, nearer spring. That should bring the cold weather back.

But although we did not get much work done, at least we were trying to 'hedge' in the right month of the year. Again over the last 12 months I have been disappointed and infuriated by the number of farmers cutting their hedges before the birds have been able to get at the berries. Indeed, many unthinking farmers are cutting their apologies for hedges so often, tight and small that they can't produce berries anyway.

It is a growing fashion to give the hedges a severe short-back-and-sides straight after harvest, and then the neighbours rush out to do the same, as if hedge-cutting has become an annual race for early tidiness. It is a sad and senseless farming fashion. Hedges do not have to be cut every year for 'efficient' farming and with the modern, fast machinery available, it can easily be done in the traditional months of January and February, without damaging crops.

It is one of my annual delights to see the fieldfares and redwings feeding from our berry-rich hedgerows. I wish more farmers would follow tradition and common sense instead of this modern fixation with tidiness. The agricultural colleges could help by encouraging young farmers to realise the wildlife value and potential of hedges – although I suspect the early flailing fashion came from the colleges in the first place.

Perhaps there should be a prize for the earliest hedge-cutter of the year – 'The Hooligan Farmer of the Year Award'. First prize would be a stuffed fieldfare. That is the only one the winner is ever likely to see.

18

Gifts From Above

ॐ

For anybody depressed by the recent anti-hunting Bill, feeling that the countryside is being taken over by townies, I have news for you – the situation is even worse than you thought. Now, after the adoration of foxes, comes the persecution of rooks.

I love rooks and I still miss the sound of the old rookery nearby that disappeared with the onset of Dutch Elm Disease. Sadly, two miles away in the Cambridgeshire village of Comberton, it would appear that some of the teachers at the village school do not enjoy these attractive, sociable and interesting birds.

In the school grounds is a small rookery, greatly enjoyed by some of the school's neighbours. Recently these same neighbours were flabbergasted to receive a letter from the Clerk to the Governors. It read:

> Every year, numerous rooks build nests in the tall trees at the front of the school. These birds overhang the parking spaces used by staff with the result that their cars are covered in bird droppings all during the spring and summer. This has become a very unpleasant problem with staff frequently having to wipe down their cars before they can get in and drive away. The bird droppings also damage the paint work necessitating frequent washing of the cars. The number of rooks using the trees has grown in recent years following the felling of a large tree in a neighbouring field, so that the problem has been getting worse.

Oh dear, what devastation – rook droppings on paintwork! When I had a swallow's nest in my garage one year, directly over my car, I simply covered the machine up and enjoyed the swallows. Evidently, unlike some people I regard the car as something useful, not as an object to worship or portray my status, or lack of it. The teachers of Comberton are lucky anyway, only having droppings on the outside – they should see what I sometimes get on the inside of my faithful Daihatsu Fourtrak. From the direction in which society is travelling I suppose that soon farmers will be obliged to put nappies on cows, sheep and even hens and farmyard muck – known also as organic manure – will be outlawed as being unhygienic.

Simply covering their cars was evidently not possible for these poor, harassed teachers, nor was walking to school, cycling or parking elsewhere: life is so hard. So, what was proposed? The school wanted to use the 'least cruel method of persuading the rooks to nest elsewhere'. The solution? To squirt the nests and birds with high pressure water jets – what a nice, friendly humane way of treating rooks. I wish I could say that all this nonsense is an early April Fools Day spoof, but unfortunately every single word is true. It has to be said too that rooks in Cambridgeshire have a hard time anyway as there are so few high trees suitable for nesting.

Perhaps the fox hunters could try the same method of fox control in the future, chasing foxes across the countryside with high-pressure water canons. It would obviously be acceptable to suburban man/and woman. For such a suggestion of rook control to come from a junior school is quite outrageous. What an example in conservation to young children and what happens when other birds offend with their droppings: house martins on house walls, or swallows in the potting shed? Knock their nests down too, I suppose? It is a case of urban-minded teachers, teaching rural children urban values. It is sad, mad, and unacceptable.

My old trumpet-blowing, pheasant-plucking, crumpet-eating friend, John Humphreys, has a useful phrase for the urbanisation of the countryside: 'These people *live* in the country, but they *think* Beaconsfield'. He is exactly right.

It was entirely by coincidence that as the 'be unkind to rooks' policy was being unveiled to the world I was reading Colin McKelvie's excellent anthology of the writings of Richard Jefferies, *Beloved Land*. In it Jefferies discusses how country children are at one with nature, how they recognise and love the flowers, trees and birds. He writes 'It will be long before education drives the natural love of the woods out of the children's hearts'. He was wrong. In Cambridgeshire it is happening now.

Just North of the City of Cambridge the process of driving out the natural love of nature is being hurried by the County Council. The people of Cambridgeshire are having a rough time with their council. For years it was an environmentally illiterate Conservative Council, now, the Lib/Lab council is showing that it can be even worse. Fine words before gaining power are followed by dubious actions afterwards. In the village of Waterbeach, made famous once through the preaching of Charles Haddon Spurgeon, the village school has built up a marvellous conservation area to allow the children to appreciate nature at first hand. There are wildflowers, grasses, a pond, great crested newts, etc. Now the council hopes to bulldoze the lot for high density bungalows. Again, what a tremendous conservation example to set for easily influenced young minds.

Last weekend I spoke at the Country Living Fair in Islington. It is a splendid example of country sanity visiting urban madness. I finished my talk by railling against all the current attacks on the countryside and saying that what we peasants really want is another Wat Tyler. One teacher in the audience was heard to turn to another and ask: 'Which party does Wat Tyler belong to?'. Yes, I really fear and grieve for the future of the British countryside, and for the education of its children, too.

19

Cock Up

❧

Over the years I have come to identify the spring with one of Britain's strangest birds; it is also one of the most beautiful. I first saw a woodcock many years ago, when as I boy I went 'beating' in the Breckland. The forests around Thetford and Brandon were, and still are, the largest area of woodland in England, and every year two uncles would go shooting there, as part of a syndicate. To earn money, and as a day out, I would go too, with various friends and associates to drive the pheasants towards the guns. Strung out in a long line we would beat the ground, shrubs and tree trunks with sticks to disturb the game and hope that it would run or fly towards the guns.

It was in those woods that I saw my first woodcock. It was a bird of mystery and beauty, flying from deep within the trees with a fast, chinking, silent flight. It was considered a great feat for a gun to shoot a woodcock, and any sucessful shot could claim £1 from each of his fellow guns.

But even at that age I could not understand why anybody should want to shoot a bird of such beauty. Its feathers were the same colours, with identical mixes and blends, as fallen autumn leaves. Seeing such remarkable birds shot was one of the reasons why, in my mid-teens, I stopped beating, and I never took up shooting. I preferred to watch wildlife, rather than shoot it. However, I am grateful to those days for giving me glimpses of the secret life of a forest: roe deer, red squirrels, a stoat in the white of true ermine and woodcock. I also have to admit, that although I do not shoot, I do like eating pheasant, which I regard as my favourite Sunday (and Christmas) dinner. They are free range, often organic birds, that have short, but free and happy lives.

Since those days I have seen many woodcock and if anything they have become more common. In February this year as I was walking at dusk from my house to the farm, one suddenly flew over the road in front of me and dropped down into a neighbour's garden. With its fast, jerky flight it was unmistakeable and as it passed it turned its head to look at me through its large brown eyes. Woodcock eat worms and other delicacies of mud, mire and soil; it is amazing that such an unattractive menu can produce such an attractive bird.

Fortunately I do not have to wait for a chance meeting to feel that little thrill of pleasure at seeing an old friend; for in a nearby wood, woodcock breed every year, and each spring, when the wood anemones and oxlips are in full bloom I sit in a tree-top hide waiting for the light to fade. Then with the western sky pink I will hear it, a frog-like croak, not on the ground where it ought to be, but up in the air, moving. It is the male woodcock 'roding'. This is his territorial flight and call and presumably, to the female sitting on eggs below, it is both melodic and reassuring. What it sounds like to a mystified frog is anybody's guess.

In the summer, with more conifer plantations growing in Britain than in the past, there are probably more breeding woodcock pairs than for many years. But although this beautiful bird seems to be more common, it retains what it has always held, a degree of mystery. If their young are in danger, or if the mother bird wants to move her chicks, how does she move them? For years, old countrymen, gamekeepers and shepherds have claimed that woodcock can carry their young. Some say they have seen them held between their thighs; others that they carry them between chin and neck, but however they carry them, there are numerous eye-witness accounts of woodcock landing

70

and their fluffy young spilling out around them. An old wood-man saw it happen along a ride in Windsor Great Park, yet most bird scientists do not believe such stories. The problem is that unfortunately much of the scientists' science is deskbound. They say that a small chick could be accidentally caught in feathers and carried a few feet before dropping out, but deliberate carry-ing is impossible. Those countrymen who have seen it are equally adamant that it is a deliberate and successful ploy. So, if it is a straightforward choice between the eye-witness account of a countryman and the considered view of a scientist, complete with PhD and 'paper' published in *Nature*, who do I believe? Why, the countryman every time of course.

I am not totally gullible, however. Before migration was un-derstood properly with the help of sane scientists and bird-ringing, people had no idea where visiting birds vanished to. In my old grandmother's Cruden's *Concordance* it says quite defi-nitely that swallows hibernate in mud, puddles and stone walls during the winter. Similarly when woodcock vanished in the spring there was a widely held view that they went to breed on the moon. Yes, the earth's first visitors to the moon were not Americans but woodcock. Even John Gay wrote:

> He sung where woodcocks in the summer feed,
> And in what climates they renew their breed:
> Some think to northern coasts their flight they tend
> Or, to the moon in midnight hours ascend.

I suppose woodcock were seen migrating during the early spring in moonlight; the next day they had vanished – gone to the moon, guided by a shaft of moonbeam. In fact I am in half a mind to believe the story now. It is a wonderful romantic notion and without the work of birdringers it would almost be logical.

There is another lovely story, too. Often there is a great au-tumn 'fall' of woodcock along the East coast of Britain, with woodcock, probably migrating from Scandinavia, arriving al-most all at the same time. Sometimes there is a similar fall of goldcrests and short-eared owls just in advance of the woodcock. This has led to the belief that both the goldcrest and the owl often act as a guide for the woodcock as it crosses the North Sea.

In Yorkshire one of the goldcrest's country names is 'Woodcock Pilot', while in some parts of East Anglia the short-eared owl is also known as the 'Pilot Owl', and the 'Woodcock Owl'. Yes, you have guessed; I want to believe these tales, too.

20

Hazy Daze

The start to spring has been dreamlike, a fusion of scent, sun, blossom and birdsong. Today's children will remember it as 'the springs we used to have'; my memory is a trifle more practical and cynical. It reminds me of the 1976 drought year and those other droughts that followed more recently.

I have never known such a mass of plum blossom, white, sweet and billowing. At dawn with the red rays of the sun melting through the mist it looks like snow. I hope late frost in April or May does not cut the fruit before it has time to form as I love English plums. If there is a fruit anywhere in the world that can match a fresh English Early River, or a firm but ripe greengage, then I have yet to taste it.

Of course the BBC weathermen excelled themselves when the plum blossom first burst. They showed a wonderful picture of apple blossom. The fact that they do not know the difference between apple blossom and plum, or the fact that one blooms well before the other should not really be a surprise; most of the time they seem quite unable to tell the difference between a warm front and a cold front either.

The bird, bees and butterflies have also been wonderful. I saw my first swallow as early as April 3rd and the bubbling, tumbling, fluting call of the willow warblers arrived along the brook last week. There have been more butterflies, peacocks, small tortoiseshells and brimstones straight after hibernation than I can remember for many years. The frogs have taken part in their amorous mass orgy in larger numbers than for a quarter of a century and reintroduced marsh marigolds are flowering for the first time since 1971.

A pair of green woodpeckers were seen one afternoon extracting goodies from an old muck heap and our CGA-sponsored hay meadow is full of cowslips. We have no orphaned or rejected lambs and the first day of the cricket season saw sun, a hard wicket and the largest crowd I can ever remember so early at Fenners.

From all this it could be assumed that my world is happy and perfect. Sadly no, for the haze the other day was not from the sun or evaporating dew, it was the smoke from the cement works over the hill, still burning toxic waste as a fuel. Plum blossom scent, blackthorn flowers, heavy metals and dioxins, I am inhaling them all. I am becoming very worried by all the bureaucrats – the ombudsmen, assorted inspectors and various health experts – supposedly employed to protect and safeguard us. The only word they seem to be able to say is 'yes'. Now, before the period of consultation over the toxic fuel has even ended, Her Majesty's Inspectorate of Pollution is saying 'yes', Rugby Cement can keep burning its 'hazardous waste', the emissions are evidently good for us. Unsurprisingly, the Regional Manager of HMIP appearing to say 'yes' is the same man who addressed a packed meeting of local residents recently. After being told of work done in America indicating that toxic waste burning is dangerous he said most helpfully: 'We are not concerned with what happens in the States'. On the question of civil service staffing to monitor the emissions he was equally helpful: 'You asked about staff and I must respond to that. Any organisation would say that they would like more staff. Yes, we have put bids in to get more staff, we cannot do our full effective regulation on the staff we have at the moment'.

What an admission. There can be toxic emissions, all over the countryside, all over me and my sheep and HMIP hasn't the staff to monitor it, although MAFF has all the staff it wants to close down small slaughterhouses which pollute nothing and offend virtually nobody. This means that if a cement works (and cement factories all over the country are now burning toxic waste – less efficiently than proper incineration plants) is given permission to burn toxic waste on a permanent basis, there will be a strong element of 'self-regulation'. By coincidence I am on a self-regulation diet. I have news for HMIP: self-regulation does not work; it never has and it never will.

When asked about heavy metals falling on the Cambridgeshire village of Trumpington, the great defender of the common man replied by saying: 'The heavy metals will have dropped out long before then'. The audience roared with laughter – sadly not with him, but at him. They were not laughing at a funny response by a comedian, but by a supposedly serious civil servant. I did not laugh; our farm is closer to the cement works than Trumpington. The heavy metals will be falling on me.

So far we are assured that the emissions are well below the required safety levels. So what is Rugby Cement planning to do? Increase the toxicity of its fuel, of course, to get the emissions closer to the limit. To me this proves that the cement company is not using the material as a fuel, it is using its kiln as an incinerator. Consequently all cement works following this path should be required to apply to their local planning authorities for a 'change of use'. Invariably they would be turned down.

Interestingly, although HMIP is taking short term decisions relating to pollution, virtually everybody realises, except it seems, HMIP, that the build-up of dioxins and heavy metals is long term. It should be monitored in soil and the fat tissue of farm animals. Amazingly, HMIP has not taken before and after samples of either. Belatedly it has started taking soil samples but animal testing? 'Testing of livestock is not within HMIP's regulatory control'; and so the comedy show goes on.

21

Absolutely Cuckoo

હૈ

In the last chapter I wrote of spring – since then there have been two signs of summer; the cuckoo has been calling from the vicinity of my cottage chimney, at first light, rattling the windows almost out of their frames – and I have shaved my beard off. The beard is an intermittent winter addition; I simply hate shaving on cold mornings. Women, or at least most of them, simply do not understand the horrors involved in shaving on a freezing morning in January. For me every January morning is cold, as I am so miserly that I have no heating upstairs; consequently I get ice on the inside of the bedroom window, and on the bathroom window, too. In such circumstances shaving has about as much appeal as listening to a six-hour party political broadcast on behalf of the Tony Blair Smiling Radiantly Party.

Normally I would welcome the cuckoo, but it came the morning after the end of lambing. Although I only have a few sheep, the responsibility is just the same as if I had hundreds. Consequently, whether you have 15 ewes or 1500, you still have to be on hand constantly at lambing time. As a result, a month of late nights and early mornings left me in great need of a lie-in.

The last ewe to lamb was our young, pure-bred Jacob, Palmnut. Her mother, Peanut, was a family pet, whose family grew up and dispersed, and so we were asked if we would give the old girl a good home. Peanut is a horrible name for a sheep, but

76

as her daughter was born on Palm Sunday we decided to keep the tradition of awful names going. Although her name is ugly, Palmnut is a very beautiful pure bred Jacob, her father being a magnificent pedigree ram from nearby Wimpole Hall.

With luck my sheep start lambing about April lst. It is a good natural time, and mother and offspring can go straight out onto fresh, growing grass. Unfortunately it seems that Palmnut did not take to the advances of Tom the Texel first time round, and so the lambing cycle this year has been longer than usual.

She finally condescended to lamb late last weekend. After the first arrival I took her into the old stable, not wanting the fox, badger or puma losses of last year. It was fortunate I was there as the second twin was stuck and I had to hoick it out manually. Putting my arm in almost up to the elbow I had to try to untangle and find various legs to ensure the lamb arrived front feet and head first. I had just been to cricket nets; it's a pity I forgot to take off my whiter than white cricket jumper.

With a bit of puffing and pulling the little black miracle finally arrived safely, with no mishap. It was a girl and she is so attractive that I will keep her for breeding. I will give her an appropriate name too – appropriate for all women. Should it be 'Trouble' or 'Late Arrival'?

After all this I collapsed into bed knowing that for the first time in weeks I could sleep through the 6.0am maternity call. The cuckoo had other ideas however, and he burst into action at 5.30. I have never before greeted my first cuckoo of the year with such warm words of welcome.

In the old days shepherds would stay out with their sheep all through lambing, living and sleeping in a shepherd's hut. Many of these huts were built on wheels so that they could be taken from field to field, or from flock to flock. They can still occasionally be seen, mostly done up as expensive pieces of garden furniture.

For some of today's large flocks the caravan has become the modern shepherd's hut. But astonishingly in certain strange parts of the country, there are people who believe that shepherds should not watch over their flocks by night, and if they do they should have nowhere special to cat-nap or make coffee.

On the edge of Dartmoor, farmer Roger Parker has some 800 ewes and to ensure safe lambing he lambs indoors, in a large shed. This year, to make the job easier and more comfortable he moved a caravan into the shed to act as his shepherd's hut. With logic that defies description, but totally in keeping with modern-day planners, the planners of South Hams District council, in Devon, told Mr Parker to remove the caravan from the shed and refused him planning permission for the new shepherd's hut on wheels. Farmer Parker was told that the caravan was not necessary and that pregnant ewes could be left on their own over night; the caravan must be removed. Mr John Eaton, Assistant Director of Planning at South Hams said: 'It does not matter whether the caravan can be seen or not. It is an area where no residential development is allowed unless there is over-riding agricultural need'. Evidently the urban–minded planners of South Hams considered lambing not to be of an 'over-riding agricultural need' – incredible.

Understandably Mr Parker was not amused: 'They expect the sheep to lamb between nine and five. It's madness. You can't even see the caravan from outside the shed. Do they expect women in maternity wards to give birth on their own during the night? It's crazy'. It is crazy too, but unfortunately it is yet another idiotic sign of the times.

As part of his protest Roger Parker was going to stand in the District Council elections on Thursday. I hope he got in. As for the planners, each one should be made to go and work on a sheep farm for a year and read the complete works of Thomas Hardy. I wonder how many of them have heard of Thomas Hardy? Or for that matter how many know which end of a sheep is which.

22

Revolting Peasants

❧

The truth is out at last: the Conservative Party is no longer the party of the countryside. Although peasants like me and bumpkins such as the redoubtable Mr Poole realised this obvious fact some years ago, it is now official. I recently had the misfortune to appear on Channel Four's 'A Week in Politics' alongside a pompous Tory MP with an enormous ego and a small majority, Mr David Sumburg, from Lancashire. The programme was about the declining support for the Tories in rural areas, their traditional strongholds. This did not seem to worry the oleaginous Mr Sumburg and before he went into the usual defence of the Conservative's appalling record he said: 'We are now an urban and suburban party. In a way we always have been. Most of us live in the suburbs . . . we live in the towns . . . the priorities have moved'. The amusing side to this of course is that the local election results demonstrated how the priorities of country people have moved, too. Throughout the heart of English Toryland, the Conservatives were booted out right, left and centre. The good news is that they deserved their cumuppance. The bad news is that for country people the new Yuppie Socialists and tedious Lib/Dems offer nothing either. We are a neglected, even persecuted, minority in our own country.

Despite their kick-in-the-pants, all we hear from Tory Central Office is that it is still only a matter of 'getting the message across clearly'. In fact the problem is too clear: the present Tories don't care, don't listen and don't change. Like me, most of my once traditional Tory friends have grievances a yard long.

My list starts with Twyford Down, the disastrous roads programme and the chaos in my local hospital. Moving on we have the outrage of the closed slaughterhouses, the nonsense of most of the £2.4 billion farming subsidies going to those farmers who need them least and the closure of coal mines, while at the same time allowing open-cast mining in Wales on Sites of Special Scientific Interest, wiping out the rare and attractive marsh fritillary butterfly in the process. Finally we have the scandal of the over-paid bureaucrats and utility big-wigs; the disgraceful destruction of our fishing industry and I only know of one person, my old father, in favour of the privatisation of British Rail, and he last went on a train in 1947. All this does not even mention Maastricht, and what are we told: it's just a case of getting the message across today, and tax cuts tomorrow; pathetic. In reality it's a case of wrong policy after wrong policy. The recent local election results represented anger. Unless things change drastically the general election will demonstrate a new Peasants Revolt. The likes of Mr Sumburg will then find that the peasants can indeed be most revolting.

Mention of television reminds me of my recent nerve racking appearance on 'Question Time'. Before the programme started I was flabbergasted. Mr Jeremy Hanley, Tory Party Chairman, thought of a possible question, but, shock, horror, he did not know the Party line, neither did his fawning personal assistant. Out came the mobile phone so that he could phone Central Office to see what he should say. Astonishing; why don't politicians say what they believe, or is that simply too difficult? Just as incredible was the colour co-ordinated socialist lady – sorry – female person, Judith Church. She couldn't shake hands with me as I arrived, she was drying her nail varnish. Oh dear. Where do the political parties dig these people up from to represent us? Needless to say the most impressive person there was not one of the three MPs, it was Chairman David Dimbleby. I wonder why people with integrity and ability are no longer attracted to Westminster politics?

I suppose the main message to come out of the VE Day celebrations was the importance of forgiveness. Despite this my old friend Gordon Beningfield tells me a story of a grudge still being held – not by a person, but by a car. His brother Roger is a very good mechanic and his hobby is collecting old Second World War vehicles. His pride and joy is a 1939 Humber Super Snipe staff car, almost certainly once used by General Sir Brian Horrocks at Intelligence Headquarters at Bletchley House.

Recently a German television crew wanted to film the car at Bletchley Park. So Roger drove down to show it off. He has owned it for 13 years, he has serviced it himself, and throughout that time it has run perfectly. On arrival the German film crew wanted him to drive through the main gate – the car would not start. Eventually it was coaxed into action, coughing and spluttering, with no visible problem. The film crew then wanted to ride inside. The car would have none of it. Once they were on board the whole throttle assembly fell to bits for no apparent reason. The lock-tabs were still tight and Roger still does not understand how it had managed to disintegrate.

The Germans went home; Roger re-assembled the throttle and the car has been running perfectly ever since. On VE Day, decked in red, white and blue it purred as new. Roger is genuinely mystified: 'It was almost as if the car was saying: "You must be joking. I'm not carrying Germans".'

On the farm to celebrate the great day we had the old hand siren out. For years after the war it was part of Britain's 'Dad's Army' early warning system. The most interesting thing about it, is the fact that for years the possession of this antiquated piece of machinery was covered by the Official Secrets Act. How the Russians must have trembled.

23

Glass War

ה

Roger Phillippo, the 'artist in glass' whose sketch of a skylark forms the centre piece of the logo adopted by the Countryside Restoration Trust, has had a visit from a dreaded environmental health officer.

For 20 years Roger has beavered away happily and healthily in his little village shop. The shop is remarkable – a small, cramped jumble, which last saw the Hoover in 1976. Roger's engraved glass is of an astonishingly high quality, beautiful, funny and original. Customers come from far and near; they know what they want and that's what they get, quality amid chaos. Indeed, part of the pleasure of going into the shop is finding objects of beauty and order in apparent total disorder. It is eccentrically, wonderfully British, a jewel in a morass of grey Euro-conformity.

Alas, the environmental health officer employed by South Cambridgeshire District Council didn't see it that way. Suddenly Roger's 'worn and threadbare' carpet became a 'trip hazard' and 'must be replaced'. All cardboard boxes must be removed 'to ensure free access for customers'. Strange, that I can get in and out of the shop all right and he needs the boxes to pack his customers' purchases.

In addition, he must 'ensure that all glass items for sale are displayed safely so as not to cause accidents'. Needless to say,

83

there has not been a single accident in the shop for the entire 20 years.

But apparently the appropriately named bureaucrat, Mrs Power, doesn't like engraved glass displayed above head height.

If he does not comply with all this nonsense, then as he carries out his engraving in the corner of this shop, he has been threatened with re-designation. He could become 'a factory'.

Roger's terse response has been to erect a new sign: 'No Tripping', to ensure that no customer suddenly dives headlong into his display cabinet.

Contrast this bureaucratic bullying of a small craftsman with the conditions sanctioned in the giant supermarkets. Recently I went to my local Tesco. Numerous items were above head height, quite safely (most things, in fact, are above head height for me – baked beans, pilchards and even lavatory brushes). I could easily have been run down by an old lady out of control with her trolley and hurled headfirst into the lavatory brushes. What would the environmental health officer have done then – closed Tesco? And of course, there were empty cardboard boxes by the till for the convenience of customers.

It's all laughable. And what makes the persecution of Roger Phillippo even more absurd is the £200 that he pays annually as a water rate for his shop. It hasn't even got a wash basin, a tap or even a toilet – they are all next door in the house. Why does he pay a water rate? For the gutter that collects rainwater from his roof, of course.

The other day I stopped at another tiny village shop. It is a traditional 'general store', stuffed full of everything from dresses to new baked bread and peaches, with vegetables in a shed at the bottom of the garden thrown in for good measure.

I am a sophisticated eater and wanted a bottle of HP sauce to have with my fish and chips. The old shop keeper didn't go to a till for the change. Instead he plunged his hand in his pockets, rattling with money.

On a good day the weight of all that cash could make his trousers fall down. Perhaps I should inform the local vice squad.

Finally, more on the Great Tory Betrayal which featured a couple of chapters ago. A telephone call came from a local reader. 'I am a Tory. I agreed with every word you wrote. Did you know that our MP is not standing next time round? You must put your name forward.'

An interesting proposition, but one which I fear would send a shudder through the present party. A rustic peasant, born, bred and working in his own constituency would be unlikely to find favour with the new breed of urban and suburban lawyers, accountants and political wheeler-dealers.

Later another friend phoned, urging me to throw my hat into the ring. To prevent Establishment 'blackballing' she suggested that I use a false name. That sounded more promising – 'Sir Jerry Wiggin', perhaps?

However, since my views are 'traditional Tory', a world away from the dogma currently pedalled by those in the dominating Born Again Cash Flow Elitist Deaf Party, I think I'd be better advised to team up with the shrewd Mr Poole and the wise Lord Deedes, with a view to re-forming the Country Party.

24

Silent Spring Becomes Soundless Summer

ぇ▲

Thirty two years ago Rachel Carson wrote her famous book *Silent Spring*. It sold like hot cakes in Britain and America and warned of an imminent catastrophe. DDT-based pesticides were entering the food chain and those at the top of the chain, the predators, were dying in their thousands. In Britain the barn owl, the peregrine, the sparrowhawk, the otter and many more birds and animals were put at risk. Songbirds too were in decline, as the insects, worms and slugs on their diets were passing on stored poisons to all who ate them. Realisation of the impending disaster came just in time; some particularly toxic chemicals were banned and slowly but surely those creatures on the brink of extinction have returned. The spring is not silent, and life has slowly returned to normal – or at least so it has appeared.

The sparrowhawk returned to my parish five or six years ago; the otter has been back for two years and I have recently seen my first barn owl in the parish since 1963. So everything in the garden would appear to be rosy. As we move into spring the dawn around my house is being greeted with a blend of many songs and there now seems to be an abundance of most garden birds (the song thrush being the notable exception). In a nearby wood the dawn chorus is rising to the level of a symphony, showing a hidden wealth of woodland birds. I have recently been to the coast too, where birds of sand, sea and marsh all seemed to be doing reasonably well.

But sadly there is still a problem. There may no longer be a silent spring, but there is a growing danger of a soundless summer. This silence is now spreading beyond the gardens, woods and spinneys whose problems have been recognised and partially solved; silence is falling like a veil over the open fields. For although many types of bird are doing well, the numbers of those depending on farmland are in steep decline.

The day I first noticed the change came seven or eight years ago. On a summer's day I was walking with the dogs along a farm track by a field of winter wheat, its green ears looking full of promise for a good harvest. There was blue sky, a warm breeze and the wild roses were beginning to bloom, but there was something missing. I stopped; what was missing? All was silence – what was it? Then it came to me, suddenly and shockingly. It was the silence, that was the problem; there should have been skylarks singing.

The music of the lark has been with me all my life; I was born in May and larksong has been almost constantly around me ever since. The skylark is the traditional bird of farmland and the open countryside, yet all I could hear was the sound of the breeze on the nearby leaves and the distant drone of traffic. I went on and once through a hedge, across grass and alongside barley, I did hear a lark, but on a walk when the music should

have been gently washing over me the whole way, l heard it briefly, just once.

Since then I have heard several larks, and set aside, that wasted land left without crops to prevent European grain mountains, is often found attractive by them; indeed in some areas it has probably saved them. According to the British Trust for Ornithology, skylark numbers have fallen by over 50 percent in the last 15 years. Other birds too have declined: the yellowhammer, the corn bunting, the lapwing, the reed bunting, the turtle dove, the yellow wagtail and even the swallow. Unlike the days of *Silent Spring* there have been few corpses to mark the arrival of Soundless Summer, so what has happened?

It would appear that this time around the changes in the countryside have been more subtle. Chemicals sprayed onto cereals and livestock are not affecting the creatures at the top of the food chain, but those at the bottom. Certain fungicides, herbicides and insecticides are removing the food supplies of insects, as well as destroying insects themselves, while herbicides are killing all weeds before they can produce the seeds that the seed-eating birds depend on. Consequently there has not been widespread starvation, an Ethiopean crisis for birds, there has been a gradual denial of food, meaning less chick survival and a steady decline in the populations.

It is almost beyond belief that it is now possible to stand at the centre of a large farm field, in the spring, without hearing a solitary skylark. For generations the skylark has been a symbol of the countryside; its song has been heard tumbling from above moor, mountain, marsh, heath, down and open field. Over the country as a whole there were millions of them, singing their song from the Shetlands to the Scillies and from St Kilda to Scolt Head. Even as I sit writing this, my mind can accurately reproduce the harmony, as it has been so constant and familiar. I remember nature walls at the village school when the 'drift' and the fields leading from it would be loud with the sound of summer larks. There would not be a single skylark but many. Often they were impossible to count – they were too high and the sky was too bright; we just accepted the constant fall of music, pure, clear and as much a part of the summer air as the scent of blossom and the sound of the swallow and cuckoo. I often remember being amazed as to how a sound so sweet and melodic could carry such long distances and how such music could flow from a bird so small, plain and brown.

The larks were there at harvest-time too as we picnicked in the fringe of shade at the field's edge. In the autumn it was still singing, as if it was in the middle of a false spring, mapping out its territory in falling song, ready for the next year. The lark has always been there: a background melody, a comfort and a joy, until that sad realisation eight years ago.

On any walk the dogs would chase larks from beginning to end. As each new chase slowed, when the lark flew higher, another would be flushed and a fresh chase would begin. I remember looking for larks' nests and heeding my father's advice: 'You will never find the nest where it lands, they always land several yards away to mislead you'. The first one I found I almost trod on; it was tucked into a cow's hoofprint and lined with hay and horse-hair. It was almost like the one remembered by John Clare, the Northamptonshire peasant poet:

There's the larks brunny (bran coloured) eggs
In an old horses foot
In a nest made of twitches
And grasses and roots
We passed it last Sunday
As I did to day
But thy foot skipt so lightly
It flew not away

The lark has given us language, too. The lark rises just before the sun and so we have 'Up with the lark' and 'Merry larks are ploughmen's clocks'. Some useful advice for a stress-free life is 'Rise with the lark and go to bed with the lamb'. Unfortunately for the lark, at one time it was also considered to be a delicacy from 'lark's tongue pie', to lark's breasts. Even the legs were a treat: 'The leg of a lark is better than the body of a kite'.

For generations the lark has been the symbol of the British countryside, inspiring poets, painters and composers. The most famous poem is by Shelley:

> Hail to thee, blithe spirit!
> Bird thou never wert,
> That from heaven, or near it,
> Pourest thy full heart
> In profuse strains of unpremeditated art.

Not so well known, but more flowing and less pretentious is 'The Skylark' of James Hogg:

> Bird of the wilderness,
> Blithesome and cumberless,
> Sweet be thy matin o'er moorland and lea!
> Emblem of happiness,
> Blest is thy dwelling-place
> O to abide in the desert with thee!

Better still is George Meredith's 'Lark Ascending':

> He rises and begins to round,
> He drops the silver chain of sound,
> Of many links without a break,
> In chirrup, whistle, slur and shake,
> All intervolved and spreading wide,
> Like water-dimples down a tide
> Where ripple ripple overcurls
> And eddy into eddy whirls . . . .

The lark is an ever present too in the writings of Richard Jefferies, Henry Williamson, H. E. Bates and the other great country writers. In music its song and the feeling of well being it gives stretches from Vaughan Williams' 'The Lark Ascending' to 'The Skylark', played by Glenn Miller.

So what has happened to the skylark, to bring silence to the heart of the country? A silence that even in the environmental gloom of the 'sixties I could never have imagined. Inevitably it is related to agriculture. Despite agricultural over-production, farming is still becoming even more intensive and every year brings new changes, together with new drugs and chemicals. The old poisons may have been banned and their lingering toxins controlled or hidden, but a new generation of chemicals is now bringing fresh problems, problems that have not yet been fully realised.

Many of the chemicals are used prophylactically; they are sprayed on as a precaution, rather than as a remedy. Modern breeds of cereals need protecting with fungicides, which remove an important food source for insects. Total insecticides too are used on a huge scale; last summer 1½ million acres were sprayed for fear of the orange wheat blossom midge. Yet in many cases the fear was groundless. Dr Nick Sotherton, Lowlands Research-Director of the Game Conservancy says: 'I have a lot of sympathy for farmers who were under considerable pressure from the farming media. But I wish they would err on the side of caution and base their spraying on facts and need. The methods used to check for a potential problem were often crude and much of the spraying was totally unnecessary as a result'.

Particularly potent insecticides are also used on rape, sileage, courgettes and aubergines. In much the same way the use of total weedkillers is now common. Although some farmers interested in wild game allow their set-aside to grow 'weeds' for the benefit of the grey partridge, a majority of farmers spray their set-aside with Roundup, a total weedkiller, as soon as they are allowed to start. That date is now April 15th which has been named by some cynics 'National Roundup Day'. It is a tragedy, for Roundup, used sensibly and responsibly, is a very useful chemical aid to farming and conservation; sadly many farmers are using it unnecessarily, without thought, out of habit, convenience and farming fashion.

The consequences are simple: the insects and seeds required as their normal diet by our once common farmland birds are gradually disappearing. Dr Dick Potts, Director-General of the Game Conservancy comments: 'The skylark has seriously declined in recent decades in the same way as the grey partridge, corn bunting and several other species. Common to all these birds is a chick diet which includes the caterpillars of sawflies which depend on traditional-ley farming. These insects have drastically declined due to a move away from undersown spring cereals and a much increased use of insecticides in the summer. Neither of these problems has yet been addressed in any measures taken by Government'.

Sadly this problem is not limited to cereal land alone, for other chemicals are now being used to control parasites in and on livestock. The chemicals linger causing considerable mortality to insects, their eggs and young. Ear tags seeped in chemicals can keep cattle insect-free for a whole summer, and all insects alighting on the animals die. Similarly the chemicals to clear an animal of worms can stay active in the animals' droppings for several days, killing some insects and invertebrates and preventing others from breeding in the pat. A neighbouring farmer told me recently: 'I know something funny is going on. Cow pats don't break up and decay any more and there are no flies on them – they stay solid for months on end'. So lapwings, larks and even swallows are now decreasing in many cattle areas where once they were common, and insects were plentiful.

The grim list of chemicals turning our summers to silence is still not at an end as there are a few that are thought to be killing the birds directly themselves. A Suffolk gamekeeper phoned me to tell me of a field of sugar beet littered with dead birds from pheasants to finches after the use of one spray. A farmer in Norfolk was quite agitated when after using a certain type of slug pellet, his largest field was littered with dead lapwings. In addition to these there is a spray used on Brussels sprouts that is believed to kill, pigeons; wild pigeons, racing pigeons and turtle doves, and a carrot spray that has been quite devastating.

The Government could have been preventing this looming disaster. Instead of set-aside it could have chosen more extensive farming to reduce crop yields. This would have lessened the use of chemicals on the land. In addition it could, and should, be breeding disease resistant crops less dependent on chemicals. Instead it has left most plant breeding to commercial breeders, tied in with the chemical companies. In addition of course, the £2.4 billion due to be paid out as EU subsidies this year should only be given to those farmers who are environmentally aware. This would mean giving far more money to the smaller and medium size farmers. It has been estimated that 4/5ths of the £2.4bn, will go to 1/5th of the farmers – the biggest, the richest, the ones who least need it and those who are doing the most environmental damage. It should also be expanding the agricultural advisory services so that farmers can be encouraged to target problems with specific, selective chemicals instead of broad band killers. For chemicals used wisely need not cause harm.

And so what is the Government doing at this crucial time? It is reducing the size of the two organisations that should be investigating and advising: the Agriculture Development Advisory Service (ADAS) and the Veterinary Inspection Service. Presumably it will only wake up once the skylark has become officially listed as an 'endangered species'

The RSPB is worried by the situation. Dr Andy Evans, the Society's Research Biologist overseeing farmland birds says: 'We are extremely alarmed at the decline of the skylark and we are about to put substantial money into researching the problem. With English nature we are also helping to fund research into the corn bunting carried out by the Game Conservancy. We want to find out what changes are happening on agricultural land. We must look for a way of integrating conservation objectives with food production'. Chris Mead of the British Trust for Ornithology agrees, and has been worried about the skylark for some time: 'Changes in farming have led to the loss of 300,000 breeding skylarks over the last 20 years. It is not the fault of the farmers – they have economic pressure on them. It is the fault of the system. Autumn planted crops are bad for skylarks. The growth is so luxuriant the young birds die – after they get cold and wet from the dew and cannot get dry. Weedkillers are so potent that the weed-seed bank is now almost depleted, so that even in newly ploughed land there is nothing to eat'.

'Skylark chicks need insects – but with insecticides there are no invertebrates available. Arable farmland is becoming totally hostile to birds. We still have many larks but their decline is serious. Rotational set-aside could help them. If it was left alone during May and June the skylarks could bring off two broods. Even the use of Roundup is not necessary; the problem is of one farmer looking over to see what his neighbour is doing.' If only common sense would return to British farming, the skylark, and a host of other once common farmland birds would return too.

As a result of our concern and after much deliberation, The Countryside Restoration Trust has chosen the skylark as its logo. It is the symbol of the farmed countryside and a sign of farming in sympathy with nature. Roger Phillippo has drawn a lark ascending, as we want to be positive, and Lyn Selby, a designer from Conwy, Gwynedd, has come up with the SOS design, to emphasise the need for urgency.

Hand in hand with this we will soon be in the position to launch our Lark Rise Farm Appeal. After the success of our first 40 acres we want to buy a whole farm to show that a thoughtful approach to farming can produce good food, rich wildlife and attractive landscape. Farming, wildlife and landscape can co-exist. Consequently we want to recreate a living landscape in which the whole countryside has wildlife. We hope to buy an over-intensively farmed farm and restore it. We will know when we have been successful when in addition to good crops we have barn owls hunting, orchids growing, and above all we have skylarks singing again over every field.

25

One Man Without His Dog

ða

I received a shock the other evening on returning to the farm; my poor old mother's pacemaker was in danger of going backwards and my sister-in-law seemed highly agitated. They had just heard the alarming news that Bramble, my beloved little lurcher, had been picked up from the side of the road by a stranger, and driven off into the sunset – he had been dog-napped. I was horrified. Was it gypsies? Was it mad vivisectionists? Or was it simply someone who recognised a good dog when he, or she, saw one? What should I do and where should I go? I felt helpless and angry; dog-napping is a mean and dreadful crime.

Not only did I feel angry for myself; I felt angry for Bramble, too. Like virtually all farm dogs his lot is a very pleasant one. Most of the time he does what he likes, when he likes, with just an occasional request thrown in to bark at the cows, or dig out a rat, requests that never need a second invitation.

His day starts off with an extension of his night's sleep. He dozes and dog-naps until mid-day. Then after another snooze he will come up to the hay meadow, or sheep field, to rest in the shade of a hedge. On returning to the farm he will visit the farmhouse to steal the food of my parents' dog and cat, plus a surreptitious wander to the bird-table to see if any tit-bits have fallen to the ground. At my brother's house the same routine of unashamed theft is followed. Then we will return home, by which time he is hungry. Following such a day he falls asleep almost immediately, waking up only to have his night-cap Bonio, after which he falls asleep again, this time flat on his back with his feet in the air – a habit he did not acquire from his master.

I have to confess that just lately the routine has altered slightly. If I was of a coarse disposition I would say that my brother's new little dog, Tess, had been on heat, and although aged over 12, the randy Bramble had been trying to get his leg over, all day and every day for a fortnight. However, as I am polite and gentle it will suffice to say that Tess has been feeling extremely friendly towards the world of late and Bramble has tried to return her friendship.

Bramble is a small, long-haired lurcher. He looks exactly like a miniature deer hound, or a mobile BBC microphone with legs. Normally he looks content and alert, with large bright eyes. After a fortnight on the tiles however, he was beginning to look rough. He had lost weight; his coat was dishevelled; Tess had bitten his ear in a lover's tiff. He was looking down-at-heel, even forlorn.

On the evening of his canine incarceration I had tried to cheer him up. I had taken him down to the field of the Countryside Restoration Trust. There I had to show a group of judges what had been achieved on Telegraph Field, as the Trust had been short-listed for Anglian Water's 1994 'Caring for the Environment Award'.

I showed them the new hedge, the new meander, the new hay meadow and the fresh signs of otters – all interesting stuff. But at the end, there was no trace of Bramble. He had vanished. I whistled. I called; nothing; I assumed that he had sneaked off for another attempted bout of love or lust.

Back at the farm there was still no sign of the roving Romeo, so I went off to imitate an over-weight geriatric trying to play tennis. On my return I was greeted with: 'Bramble's been stolen'. Apparently the dog-napper had been seen: an elderly woman had stopped her car and ushered Bramble aboard, as he had been minding his own business and thinking of his next romantic manoeuvre.

Then came a telephone call. The dog-napper had been spied in the next village. She had stopped at a farmhouse to get the poor battered, starving dog a drink. She had been told where Bramble lived and that he normally looked like that, but no, it was an ill-treated, abandoned stray: she was taking Bramble to the dogs' home. 'She's always doing this', the informer added. Bramble in a dogs' home – what canine horror and humiliation.

I phoned the Wood Green Animal Shelter at Heydon, near Royston. Sure enough they had just received a little lurcher. 'And was it wandering about lost sir, without a name?'. 'He doesn't wear his name, to prevent him being stolen by gypsies,' I replied, 'and he wasn't lost. He knows everybody and everybody knows him. He's been in the papers, he's barked on the radio and he's going to be on television. He couldn't be lost'. There was a pause: 'Oh no. He's not the dog who's going to be on "One Man and His Dog?" and who's being paid in Bonios, is he?', the man asked in disbelief. 'He is,' I replied. 'You have a kidnapped star'.

I roared over to the dogs' home where a traumatised Bramble greeted me with a grin, a bark and a wagging tail. He has stuck to me like a leech ever since, romance forgotten. A charge of £25 can be made for the return of a handed-in dog; fortunately the charge was waived.

This whole worrying incident has raised an important social issue. How do we survive and avoid old ladies wandering loose in the countryside? I have come to the conclusion that they should be radio-tagged and numbered so that we know exactly where they are, who they are and what they are doing. Then, when they get too near we can all take cover. I am also having Bramble put on the National Pet Register, in case the dog-lifter strikes twice. He will be numbered and if handed in again he will be quickly returned home. I suppose I could also give him a doggie T-shirt bearing the message 'Please Leave me Alone – I normally look like this'. Details of the Register can be obtained from The National Pet Register, Heydon, Royston, Herts SG8 8PN.

26

SOS – Save Our Swallows

To me one of the most important birds of an English summer is the swallow. 'One swallow doesn't make a summer', but a summer without a swallow would be unthinkable. The swallow is as much a part of summer as cricket, strawberries and cream, the cuckoo, the village flower show, the skylark and sweet-smelling roses. Nearly all country people regard it as a friend and it features in folklore, the words of writers such as Gilbert White and John Clare and in the work of numerous artists including Thomas Bewick and Archibald Thorburn.

As a boy I remember as many as 14 swallows' nests around our traditional family farm. The first swallow of spring was always greeted with excitement: it really did mark the end of winter and heralded the return of the sun. Even at that time I was amazed by the swallow's annual journey. How could a bird so small and fragile travel thousands of miles over sea, mountain, desert and plain to get to the southern most tip of Africa? It seemed an incredible journey. And then, after a winter of African warmth, the little bird would return to Britain to breed.

Over recent years I have made that same journey many times. I have seen European swallows at Cape Point, where the Indian and the Atlantic Oceans meet and where, looking south, the next great continent is the Antarctic.

In March I have seen them in their thousands, hawking over the surface of the great Zambezi river for insects. Then, a fortnight later a pair has arrived back in our garage. I have seen them hunting around elephants and giraffe and flitting through thorn scrub where cheetah have been resting. On the banks of the Tana River I remember watching them with George Adamson and he too wondered at their incredible journey, their beauty and their powers of navigation. He was interested in so much more than his beloved lions.

It was, and still is, an 'incredible' journey; a migration involving many thousands of miles each year. How do they do it? Do they follow the stars? Do they recognise the wind, the mountains or the sea? Can they detect magnetic fields? The scientists cannot agree and we will never know. All I know is that for years, swallows that travelled across Africa returned each year to our garage, barn, tractor shed, stable and hen houses. Sometimes the same birds will return to the same garage or barn for year after year, clocking up incredible distances.

Like many others I believe they follow the stars; although they travel mostly during the hours of daylight, I suspect they use the stars at dusk and dawn like a map, with a little directional help from the sun for good measure. But each year, however they travel, with or without the stars, their navigation brings them back to the exact spot they left the previous autumn.

The nests of mud would be under the eaves, on rafters, or simply stuck to a wall. The eggs were always safe inside because of the soft lining of feathers, hay and horse hair. Swallows were everywhere, hawking over the hay meadows and wheat fields after flies and insects. They would swoop over water, sometimes rippling the surface to drink or skim up a struggling insect. At cricket matches the birds would be patrolling the outfield and at picnics they would be flying along the hedgerows. In good weather they would fly higher after flies, but as soon as they flew low we knew that bad weather was on the way. To many old farmers and labourers the swallow was an accurate forecaster of the weather; who needs Michael Fish when there are reliable, natural weather guides?

Some years each pair would rear two broods of young, while in good, warm years three was the norm. Recently I had a letter from a lady claiming that last year she had a pair that brought off five broods, a remarkable achievement. Sometimes we have had to help the adult birds bring off their broods, returning chicks to their nests and once putting up a modified bird box when a nest containing young collapsed completely. More recently we have kept a constant vigil for magpies and sparrowhawks, throwing things at them to move them on and away from the youngsters just out of the nest.

Two years ago one of the adults disappeared. We suspected a sparrowhawk, or a speeding car. The one remaining parent flew all the hours of daylight to get her brood off - she succeeded – but they did not leave until the beginning of October.

The latest I have seen a swallow feeding was in late November over the Great Ouse at St Ives (Cambs). Many times stragglers are still flying over in October. One year after the nearby brook flooded swallows and house martins were taking insects floating in the flood; some even landed at the water's edge to feed on drowned bugs and beetles.

One of the most remarkable examples of feeding came during a cold, damp spell in May. A pair of swallows had young but there seemed to be no insects. The swallows were wiser. Our sycamore tree was flowering and was full of insects attracted by the scent. For the whole damp, dull period the swallows hunted in and around the sycamore tree and nowhere else. The sycamore gave them food for their young until the warmth returned. Many conservationists do not like the sycamore, claiming that it is alien and does nothing for wildlife. I have just planted another: to me it is the swallow tree, providing food at a vital time.

Sadly, since the days when 28 swallows made our farm their home, numbers have steadily fallen. During the drought years of the late Eighties and early Nineties we had many chick deaths through sheer heat. Because of this the veterinary medicine manufacturers 'Intervet' sponsored an insulated roof on our barn to lower the temperature. One pair hung on until last year when no swallows bred: it was the first time in living memory that the farm had been swallowless.

Although the swallow population is known to fluctuate, there does now seem to be a steady decline. In the last 25 years the summer population of England, Scotland and Wales has decreased from 750,000 pairs to 500,000. It is an alarming drop and the signs are that it will continue. At one time it was thought that the disappearance of swallows was caused by the increasing size of the Sahara Desert or that bad weather on migration caused enormous crashes. However, there is growing evidence that the cause could be much nearer home.

Over much of Britain mixed farming is a thing of the past. Swallows love areas of cattle and sheep, as the flies that accompany livestock, pasture and cow-pats create abundant food. Where cattle numbers have declined so has the food of the swallow.

Cereal land too could still supply insects, but all too often these days total insecticides can be sprayed over summer corn, removing the swallow's source of food almost completely. Last summer 1½ million acres were sprayed to to protect wheat crops from the ravages of the orange wheat blossom midge. Unfortunately, too often all species of insects were wiped out by the non-selective insecticides used; it created a virtual food desert for the swallow here in England. Ironically when comparitive tests were carried out on the yields of sprayed and unsprayed areas of wheat, little difference was in fact found.

Even in livestock areas the story is not good. The increasing amount of grass cut throughout the summer for sileage is removing breeding habitat for insects, and a new generation of chemicals for animals, aimed at worms and flies, can kill all insects and bugs in and on the cattle throughout the summer. In addition the same chemicals can remain active in droppings for several days and it is thought that insects relying on cow pats for food and breeding conditions are being affected. Consequently circumstantial evidence points to a chemically created crisis – the swallow is simply having its source of food removed.

In addition to all this, many farmers are becoming 'tidy': ponds and puddles are being filled in and so the swallow is finding it increasingly difficult to find mud with which to nest build. New farm buildings are also being built bird-proof, denying the swallow access.

This tidiness has spilled over to ordinary householders, too; most gardens now have no areas of useless mud and the garage and the garden shed are kept closed. The poor swallow has no nesting material and no nest site. It is a sad, sad, state of affairs and urgent action must be taken before it is too late.

Because of all this the Government must give financial inducements to farmers to farm in a more traditional way as it does already in Environmentally Sensitive Areas. Farmers should receive payments for keeping their livestock numbers down, to prevent over grazing, and for growing hay, cut in July, and not sileage, which can be cut periodically from April until November. Sileage is very destructive and wipes out ground-nesting birds and destroys habitat for breeding insects.

Already the Government is paying farmers over £2.4 billion pounds per year in E. U. subsidies. At the moment this money goes mainly to cereal growers and four fifths of the total goes to one fifth of the largest and richest farmers, making them richer still and helping them to become even larger. This money should be re-directed to encourage mixed farming, and environmentally friendly farming. Not only would this help the swallow, but also a wide variety of wildlife and landscapes. It could also help to keep people working on the land as mixed farming requires more labour than specialist farming.

Urgent research by the Agriculture Development Advisory Service (ADAS) and English Nature must be funded by Government into the new breed of cattle wormers and fly sprays, to establish their effect on overall insect populations. Research must be widened to cover the effect of insecticides on the food requirements of all farmland birds including the swallow, skylark, lapwing, tree sparrow, corn bunting, turtle dove,

English partridge, etc. If a link is established, more environmentally friendly products must be developed.

The Government should produce a list of wildlife-friendly cereal sprays and veterinary products so that those farmers wanting to farm sympathetically and responsibly can do so. Astonishingly MAFF has no such list at present, neither has ADAS, LEAF (Linking Environment And Farming) or FWAG (the Farming and Wildlife Advisory Group). Some of these groups receive funding from the agrochemical industry and LEAF has chemical company representatives serving on its Executive Gouncil.

At the moment ADAS is shrinking and its services are expensive. The Government should expand this potentially important advisory service and make it free and available to all farmers. It should be a source of readily available, *impartial* advice. At the moment farmers are seeking advice from the chemical companies themselves.

Farmers should try to use less chemicals and they should use them only when a problem is looming. They should not be used prophylactically over the whole farm. Livestock farmers ought to avoid using worm boluses (long lasting pills). They are an excuse for lazy, bad management and they prevent natural immunity. White wormers should be used such as 'Panacur' and the types should be rotated to avoid a resistance building up. 'Vetrazin' is effective against fly strike on sheep and its use is allowed in organic flocks. A good environmental sheep dip to protect against scab is 'Bayticol'. An acceptable fly and lice killer is 'Spot On', another chemical allowed in organic herds.

On our farm we have stopped using Ivomec products. Many of them are long-lasting and superficially attractive to farmers (it was attractive to us before doubts developed). Some of the products contain 'avermectins'; many conservationists believe that these chemicals may be helping to cause a long term decline in insect populations. I will need far more reassurance, from independent sources, before I would use these long term wormers and fly-killers again.

Ponds and wet areas should be left, both as good insect breeding areas i.e. swallow food, and as providers of mud for nest making.

Old buildings should be left with windows or doors open for swallow access.

New buildings should be fitted with eaves, together with wooden boards and artificial beam ends to encourage nesting.

Modern machinery sheds should be fitted with false beams or rafters for nesting sites; access windows should be constructed. Keep bird-free zones to a minimum.

The ordinary householder can also take action to help the swallow. Leave the windows of garages and garden sheds open to allow access for swallows.

Cover the car, or park it outside to avoid the droppings.

Ensure that a puddle or the garden pond has an area of mud for nest building.

Modify a nest box or a hanging basket in case of nest collapse. Fix how and where you can, when needed.

Try putting in artificial beam ends under house or shed eaves to create additional nesting sites – this can also attract house martins.

Before the swallows arrive check old nests for mite infestation. If 'lousy' sprinkle lightly with Ruby Stable Insecticide Powder, obtainable from Brian G. Spencer Ltd, Common Lane, Fradley, Litchfield, Staffs. (Telephone: 01543 2628820). In hot years a mite population explosion can occur, causing the young swallows great discomfort, even jumping from the nests long before flight is possible – in extreme conditions, Ruby Stable Insecticide should be used again, on the nest and young birds.

The most important action for swallows is the simplest. If you have swallows, help and encourage them. Tell your friends, neighbours, small-holders and farmers to follow your good example.

Help Save Our Swallows before it is too late.

27

'Rights' and Responsibilities

Last year I made myself a promise. This year I broke it; I visited the Stoneleigh Car Boot Sale, known also by some as the Royal Show. It was an immensely depressing experience, as every year it gets less and less like an agricultural show. I could have bought new windows for my hovel, cuddly toys, furniture from India, paintings created with an iron, not a paint brush, and any number of 'kitchen devils'. It was so awful that I left before I had seen a cow, or even a tractor, although I did see an ostrich and a flock of top-of-the-range Jaguars for sale; it is good to know that some of those huge subsidy cheques are being catered for. I also saw abundant signs that the farming establishment regard agriculture merely as an industrial process, and nothing more. For the small farmer, the traditional farmer and the enlightened farmer, Stoneleigh is a place to be avoided.

I went to the car boot sale to take part in a countryside forum organised by *The Field* magazine, where the dominant subject was 'access'. That was depressing, too. The arguments against 'open access' are overwhelming – except on the large industrial farms that have got nothing to protect – but I suspect that when we get a new Labour Government, the perpetually grinning Mr Blair will listen to the Ramblers rather than to reason. It will be populist rather than honest. Incidentally, how does Mr Blair manage to speak while grinning inanely at the same time? I have tried, but find it impossible to keep dry when not wearing a bib.

The facts are simple: 91% of the population is urban and sub-urban, and a large section of that 91% can't tell the difference between a cowslip and a cowpat. Because of this, access in sensitive areas of the countryside should be 'controlled' and available to those people who are interested or educated in the ways of wildlife and the countryside. The interests of the young otter, the flowering orchid and the skylark's nest dictate caution and care, rather than political slogans about 'rights', 'freedoms' and 'open access'. It is about time too that politicians realised that for every 'right' there should be a 'responsibility'.

We welcome visitors to our farm as we want to see the gap between town and country closing. But we make one or two requests, the most important being that dogs are kept on leads. Bramble knows what he can do, when and where, but many strange dogs with new sights, sounds and smells become uncontrollable. So what happens to our modest request? Our Countryside Commission notices, 'Please keep Dogs on Leads', are forever being ripped down and broken into tiny pieces. I do not understand it. Incidentally, what is the collective noun for a group of ramblers? A whine!

The great unanswered question about access is: who pays for accidents? At the moment the landowner faces liability, but why should he, or she? If a visitor, unaware of the delights of country living, arrives in a field and slips base over apex in a cowpat, relieves himself over the electric fence, falls out of a tree or gets tossed by a bull, thanks to the antics of his free-roaming dog, surely it is the visitor who should take out insurance not the farmer. One of the first things the new Secretary of State for Agriculture, Fisheries and Food, the aptly named Mr Hogg, should do, is to rule that with access comes responsibility, and part of that responsibility is for every rambler, walker and visitor who wants compensation for stings, bruises and bites, to be insured. The ordinary farmer, carrying out his work responsibly should be relieved of all liability.

What will happen if present trends continue, I wonder? To ensure public safety in the countryside, and to create jobs, the number of Environmental Health Officers will be doubled. Where access exists, landowners will be required to scoop up cowpats daily, fit all passing pigeons with nappies, remove all branches from trees, hoover up every fallen leaf in the autumn and treat the farm dog for halitosis. It sounds absurd, but as sure as day follows night, in the present atmosphere of unreality and madness some of this nonsense is bound to become reality.

Why is there yet another new Secretary of State at MAFF? I am sure that Mr Douglas Hogg is a very nice man for an Etonian and a Barrister (there are so many of them in the Tory Party, did Central Office get a job lot?), but why did Mrs Shephard and Mr Waldegrave go before they had even got their feet properly under the desk?

Because the top dog moves so frequently, it means that for a considerable time MAFF has been effectively controlled not by the politicians, but by the civil servants, urban ones at that. Consequently the whole emphasis over recent years has been on production and production control, rather than good farming with conservation; conservation has become just an inconvenient piece of tinsel, to be waved about at convenient moments. As I understand it, most of the top MAFFIA bureaucrats are urban, and would be hard pushed to recognise a muckheap from a mole-hill. I am reliably informed that the accents of rural Devon, Norfolk and Yorkshire are unknown in the higher echelons, the prevailing accent is urban Essex, in fact Dagenham. MAFF is run by Dagenham Man. Perhaps the Trade and Industry Department should be supervised by a reclusive crofter from the North West tip of Tiree.

As soon as I met Gillian Shephard, when she was Agricultural supremo, she was moved. A fortnight ago I arranged to see William Waldegrave; now he has gone. I think I had better refrain from trying to ear-tag Mr Hogg; we need an over-due dose of agri-continuity.

28

The Lark Descending

❧

When I wrote about the skylark in April, it evidently struck a chord with many people. Over 600 letters poured in and amazingly letters are still arriving. In addition there were numerous telephone calls and even personal visits. Two things have become abundantly clear as a result. The skylark is one of Britain's best loved birds and very many people are worried by its sudden and continuing decline.

Letters have come from all four home countries, as well as from Ireland. In a few areas larks and other farmland birds are still in their old numbers, but generally I have read and heard of decline, worry and almost silent skies.

Farmers have written, concerned about their disappearing birds; ordinary country people have complained about their losses and several townspeople have described returning to old holiday haunts to find a changed and almost deserted land. A farmer from the south explained how sileage and new methods have allowed him to double the numbers of his stock; but he has lost his wildlife and he is now questioning both his methods and the chemicals that he is using.

A correspondent from Wales tells how the decline in the lark has been matched by a noticeable fall in the number of insects. Summer car journeys once covered her car windscreen wlth dead insects; now those same journeys are achieved with clean glass and there is little larksong at the end of the journey.

One fine old countryman drove all the way from Lincolnshire to show me photographs of his once favourite walk, along the banks of the River Welland. Originally there were wildflowers and grasses galore; skylarks were plentiful, as were meadow pipits, English partridges and pheasants. Then the National Rivers Authority started mowing the bank twice a year. He found smashed eggs and the birds lost their cover. The photographs show a wide river bank cut short like a lawn. The NRA, which is supposed to support conservation has now compromised and cuts the banks just once a year. But the damage has been done and a host of birds have gone. Since his visit other complaints about bank cutting have come in and I have seen many examples myself. One of the worst was on the River Nar in Norfolk in late May. Why the NRA does not cut its river banks in late summer, or even every other year, as comnmon sense suggests, is a mystery.

Several correspondents have pointed out a sudden dramatic fall in the population of the ubiquitious house sparrow, which seems in imminent danger of ceasing to be ubiquitous. These reports caused me to stop and take stock of the sparrow population in our farmyard, and sure enough it has tumbled too, in the last two years. But at least we have some; a friend who farms in the next village has lost his house sparrows completely. This loss is at a time when most people assume that the only sparrow under pressure is the now rare tree sparrow.

Because of our disappearing sparrows I have even had a change of heart. A pair of sparrows decided to squat in one of my artificial house martin nests. I was about to issue an eviction notice, but decided to let them stay after all.

There have been horror stories of the declining number of larks, linnets and thrushes having to contend with rampant magpies and sparrowhawks. In addition there have been the usual tales of irresponsible farmers spraying in high winds and of spilt chemical pellets left littering the ground.

109

One lady who telephoned found a number of dead hedgehogs around the edge of a field; empty slug pellet boxes pointed to an obvious cause. Another caller reported more dead bodies after the application of pellets which he assumed to be slug pellets. The field was covered with dead worms that had simply come to the surface in large numbers and died. Chemicals killing worms – the farmer's and the soil's best friends? The obvious question also needs to be asked: what happened to any birds eating the worms?

Many people have also suggested that the article was long overdue. It was, but the response to it raises an interesting question. There is obviously a very serious problem developing in the British countryside, with the loss of wildlife on a massive scale. All the indications point to agriculture and to a new generation of crop sprays and veterinary applications, as well as to habitat destruction and thoughtless farming. So why was it left to me, a simple country peasant, to put my head up above the parapet? Where were FWAG, LEAF, ADAS, the Ministry of Agriculture, the NFU, the farmimg Press and the agri-chemical industry itself? They were all in a far better position than me to name names and ask for action. So why the silence?

In fact only two organisations have stood up to be counted; the British Trust for Ornithology and the Game Conservancy, and the Countryside Restoration Trust is joining them. I suppose it is another sorry story of not wanting to step out of line and/or keeping an eye on the sources of funding. LEAF is an interesting case in point. It is supposed to be encouraging environmentally friendly farming and is full of fashionable agri-jargon about 'integrated crop management'. But it can't even produce a list of environmentally friendly chemicals for interested farmers; this is hardly surprising as it has the NFU, MAFF and some of the large chemical companies represented on its Executive Council.

To their credit, two of the the large chemical companies approached me, and the Countryside Restoration Trust, for discussions about our concerns. And we have accepted invitations from both DowElanco and Rhone Poulenc. DowElanco went even further and issued guidelines for the spraying of the dreaded Orange Wheat Blossom Midge to try to ensure that spraying only took place when there was a proven problem. But surely it is time for the Ministry of Agriculture to get its act together and launch a major enquiry into the crisis facing some of our farmland wildlife? We need action now, not sorrow when it is too late.

29

Needing the Dough

ॐ

The present day harvest is like a modern mechanical miracle. Few people are involved and the 'harvest home' is not accomplished by hordes of sweating farm labourers working from dusk to dawn; it is achieved by a few men and women working in comfort with modern technology. Armchair tractor drivers with all mod-cons pull huge grain trailers, and combine harvesters the size of tanks devour the crops whenever the 'moisture content' allows. Even that is not the complete story, for if the grain in the ear fails to dry sufficiently during a wet summer, then the combines will still roll while the corn is damp, and driers will be used to ensure that the crop is dry and that it will not rot.

The whole process is one of noise and speed, dust, dirt and high technology. At the end of the old harvests there was a feeling of relief and achievement, and all those involved celebrated at a party, with much merriment, eating and drinking; the 'horkey' was a feature of the farming year. We still have a horkey on our small farm, when 'all is safely gathered in'. Sadly on many farms the horkey has become yet another lost tradition; all that happens now when harvest stops is that ploughing starts and the combines are put away until next year. All they will want between the end of one harvest and the beginning of another is an after harvest service.

But the old harvest and the new, still have one thing in common, the end product: wheat. That still means food, biscuits, cereals, flour and bread. The task of milling, baking and delivering new loaves has been highly mechanised too, so much so that many modern people have almost lost the link between harvest and food. They see the large combines in the field and the piles of bread in the supermarket and they fail to realise or understand the relationship between the two.

At times they can hardly be blamed as some modern bread is a sad imitation of the real thing. It is bland, soft and almost tasteless; even Bramble my dog puts his nose up and would rather go hungry. Fortunately, however, some small, traditional bakeries remain; we get our bread from a tiny back street bakery on the outskirts of Cambridge and there the old smells and traditions remain, with real hot crusty bread. It is served by real people too, with a smile and a comment. It wlll be a sad day if and when all the traditional, small shops disappear because of undercutting by the large, impersonal super-stores. I prefer small shops and shopping with service and a smile.

I love new-made bread. For years, when I was a boy, my mother made all our bread. It was wonderful stuff with thick crispy crust and somehow the warmth from the stove and the smell of the bread was evocative of those hot open fields and harvest. When she kneaded the dough it was still warm, but the kitchen smelt slightly musty, of yeast. I can smell it now. When the tins with their new loaves emerged, I was the first in the queue for a crust. When she made cottage loaves, with no tins, there was even more crust. The overall result was that our bread consumption rocketed. Although nearly 80, she still occasionally makes bread, filling the farmhouse with that welcome, warm smell of new loaves. The bread itself is as good as ever. A cousin has caught the habit and I am trying to develop the skill of visiting at the exact time when the loaves come out of the oven.

What brought out the taste of our traditional bread still more was the fact that we often used home-made butter. There was no question of fat-free, sunflower spread or margarine. We had proper butter made from the the top of the milk, full cream. The butter was soft, yellow and flavoured with salt, a filling for a sandwich was not required when the bread was new; it was bread and butter turned into a feast.

Even now we sometimes have schools visit the farm. We show them the grain bins, to explain where wheat, flour and bread come from. We then milk Cowslip the Jersey house-cow to show them where milk comes from and how the cream floats to the top. We then make butter. We explain of course how Jersey cows are famous for the richness of their milk and how they are about the most good natured of cows. To prove the point they are allowed to stroke Cowslip, and they usually give her a round of applause. She is a lovely old cow. I brought her to the farm as a new-born calf, in the back of my car, from a beautiful, traditional dairy farm with a large pedigree herd of Jerseys. Now, six calves later, she is almost part of the family. I don't have to fetch her from the field for milking, I simply call her name.

We have a small modern butter churn, a glass jar with paddles rotated by a handle. As the cream is beaten into butter we get the children to recite a little verse that has been said by generations of watching children, dating from the time when butter was made on nearly every farm. It goes:

Come butter come.
Come butter come.
Peter's waiting at the gate,
Waiting for some buttered cake,
Come butter come.

Once the butter forms we tell the children that we are going to do to the butter what they do before they go to bed. This creates a problem for them, as butter has no teeth or hair; the idea of washing butter does not occur to them. We then wash it with cold water to get rid of the excess fat and buttermilk, then squeeze it with butter pats, add salt and 99.9% of all the children who have ever visited the farm claim that it is the best bread and butter they have ever tasted.

Friends on the edge of the fens still grind their wheat for bread-making flour in an old windmill. Considering the technology of the age the windmill is every bit as remarkable as the combine harvester. The smell and the gentle noise seems to be in harmony with nature; the wind-whistling sails, the creaking timber, the soft working of hard wooden cogs and the grinding sound of stone on stone as the corn is ground into flour. Sadly, a modern mill, with lorries, dust, electric engines and noise seems to be alien, a sign of the industrialisation of both farming and food. By comparison the windmill seems a natural part of a more friendly world, and a more peaceful world.

30

Fire

ễ

It has been a hot harvest: good for the quality of the grain and good for getting the combining done; but for us it became rather too hot. We had about five minutes to go to the end of harvest. I suddenly smelt burning. 'Funny,' I thought, my neighbours must be burning something strange on their bonfire. We unloaded the combine, on the move, and then I got another, stronger whiff. 'Funnier still,' my brain told me, working at its maximum capacity: 'We are now a long way from my neighbours' garden; why such a strong smell of burning?'. As I pulled away with the tractor and grain trailer I didn't have to strain to see exactly where the bonfire was – it was on the combine, with flames lapping all around the engine.

Standing corn; acres of tinder dry stubble; FIRE! My brain suddenly went into automatic pilot. 'FIRE! STOP THE ENGINE,' I screamed at my brother. I hit the tractor's manual throttle to slow and leapt off, leaving the tractor and the grain trailer still in gear. As I ran in a northerly direction, the tractor continued in a southerly direction.

John, my brother, scrambled off the combine and kindly handed me the canister of water to fight the fire. Faster than Jonathan Edwards can say 'Hop, step and jump', I was on top of the combine slopping water onto the flames – meanwhile the tractor continued to head south. With the last of the water the flames died, but with the steam came more smoke as dust smouldered on the hot engine. Suddenly fire erupted again. There was nothing for it – no, not that – I ripped my shirt off and frantically beat at the flames. 'Take the tractor to fetch water,' I shouted to John. Tractor? What tractor? The tractor had disappeared. It was just ploughing straight through a hedge into our neighbour's wheat. John set off like a gazelle in pursuit, a very old, fat gazelle. Scrambling through blackthorn and briars he climbed into the back of the tractor cab to pull the stop knob. I was standing like king of the firemen on the combine with my tanned face and arms in stark contrast to the graceful lines and lily-white colour of my exposed stomach. I have never been a follower of fashion, colour coordination, or diets.

Fortunately my sweaty T-shirt did the trick; the fire was out. It has been a close shave. We finished harvest the next day after various pipes and pieces had been replaced on the combine. A new loaf of bread at the baker's can never quite show what went into its production.

I haven't needed a ladder to pick my Early River plums this year. The tree is so loaded that in places the branches touch the ground. My greengage tree is almost as good. Needless to say with all this wonderful English fruit around, the supermarkets are still full of European rubbish. It just shows how divorced from reality both the supermarket buyers and the customers have become; how can they stock and purchase this junk fruit? It

is not an anti-European matter, it is a matter of fact and taste that British plums are in a class of their own. The perfect plum is a 'temperate' fruit, not a Mediterranean one, a fact that is evidently beyond the comprehension of the superstore managers.

I suppose they go for the inferior fruit because of the guaranteed supply. The point that good English fruit depends on the season, the weather and the frost is not understood. They want supply, so guaranteed French rubbish gets the contract. Last year I bought French greengages by mistake: the first bite told me exactly where they came from. I could not believe that such abominations could turn up for sale even in my local village stop. I urged Rodney, my local shopkeeper, to put a health warning on them.

In a nearby village the small general stores received a visit from 'Trading Standards' the other day. The shopkeeper was informed that he must put 'country of origin' on all his fruit. The problem was quickly solved; he put 'Foreign' stickers on his coconuts.

The wonderful plum harvest is a mystery. The amount of springtime blossom was astonishing. But then we had late frosts that should have wiped out the crop completely; but somehow the fruit escaped. By comparison I recently visited an excellent vineyard in Suffolk, where the owner has lost 80% of his grape harvest because of that same frost. It is a shame, because the wine from Giffords Hall, near Bury St Edmunds, is superb, and any reduction in the number of bottles produced will be a tragedy. A few years ago English wine was diabolical, marginally better than anti-freeze and worse than vinegar; now, however, there are some superb English wines that can compete with the best European vintages.

By coincidence, Giffords Hall is owned and run by John Kemp who for many years was Social Services Correspondent for *The Daily Telegraph*. Several years ago he dropped out of journalism for the 'Good Life'. I hadn't seen or heard of him for 20 years; I was glad to stumble into him in his new incarnation; his wine was a revelation. Sadly I bought almost his last three bottles of last year's 'medium'. If I was related to Oz Clarke (*The Daily Telegraph*'s excellent and amusing wine correspondent) I would write that its 'bouquet' was of tropical fruits – mango with a scent of citrus. The first sip brought a taste explosion, cool, fruity, yet both bitter and sweet. At the back of the throat there was a sudden second burst of grape, sun and subtlety'. However, I am not related to Oz Clarke. I am a country bumkin; to me the wine's smell was, unsurprisingly, of grapes; each one crushed by the feet of John Kemp. He told me that after my purchase. By comparison French wine smells remarkably like an ancient urinal I once had the misfortune to wander into in the back streets of Nîmes. The taste too was excellent; it made the average German Hock seem as dull as ditchwater. I hope this year's 20% is as good.

31

Harvest Home

&

The British countryside is becoming a sad place. One by one its customs and traditions are being eroded away, until finally they will all disappear. Part of the problem is, I suppose, that we are living in an urban/industrial dominated society. In such a society even farming has been turned into an industrial process; as a consequence many farmers and landowners, particularly of the non-hunting, shooting, fishing variety, have become little more than land managers or factory foremen.

Gone is the romance of living and working on the land; gone are the traditions and celebrations of the seasons and gone are

120

the laughter, the enjoyment and the sense of fulfilment that once went with traditional farming.

The disappearance of our traditions and celebrations is really very sad. At the present rate of progress, by the year 2000 there will only be two left, the harvest festival and the carol service. Even then there will be trendy vicars urging us to remember the harvest of the inner-city, placing P45s, empty cider bottles and discarded syringes where there were once sheaves of wheat and loaves of bread. No doubt the politically correct will also demand changes to the carol service: it will become a 'multi-cultural' event, with earnest exhortations to Allah and Shiva. To salve the social consciences of the misguided, punch and mince pies will have been replaced by pea soup and tea in polystyrene cups for the benefit of any passing dossers, drunk or drop-outs.

To try and reverse the social flow it really is time that those of us who live in the country should begin to show that we actually like it; that we are proud of our past, and of our present. We should start celebrating our good fortune; we should get back to celebrating the seasons and the farming practices that go with them: bring back the Maypole, 'beating the bounds', Morris Men and the Horkey.

The Horkey is especially important at this time of year, but now, sadly, even some of the farming community have no idea what it is – perhaps they should simply celebrate the arrival of the IACS cheque. The Horkey was, is, and should always be, a gigantic knees-up and blow-out to celebrate the end of harvest. Everybody with links to the land should celebrate harvest home. Do not be misled; despite the free-market, city slickers, high-tech mania and the commuter colonisation of the countryside, the most important job and function on the planet remains that of growing food and gathering it in safely.

Once harvest home was celebrated in style on virtually every farm in the country; now, the day harvest stops, ploughing, cultivating and drilling begins: it is just another day at the farm-food factory. It should also be said for the benefit of the environmentally illiterate land manager, that the day harvest ends, the senseless out of season massacring of our hedgerows also continues.

I have always loved harvest, and I still do; for me this makes the passing of the Horkey even more miserable. Harvest today is faster, noisier and dirtier than in the old days – except for the boy that was once put in charge of the chaff on the old threshing machines – but there is still a sense of anticipation and urgency. Then, on the last day, as the combine is driven out of an empty field, back into its shed for another year, I always feel thankful, happy and elated – whether the harvest is good or bad, and whether the grain bins are over-flowing or half empty. It means that we have done our best for another year: the farming year is at an end. Yes, a new one does begin again straight away, but at least let's pause, reflect and celebrate.

The Horkey was once exactly that – it was a celebration for harvest home, when all those who had taken part, and their families, could eat, drink and be merry. But now the rush and tare has meant Horkey beware, the great harvest supper has almost disappeared. Chris Knights, that larger than life character in East Anglia with one of the most impressive farms in the country both for wildlife and food production says: 'We can't have a Horkey for harvest – our harvest never stops, it goes on all the year'. His grain harvest stops, but his vegetable production line is a continuous process. A near neighbour of his grows cereals, but he also grows two crops of potatoes, one after the other; his second crop is planted in July and harvested in October or November as supermarket 'new potatoes'. Not much chance of a Horkey there. Richard Mayall farms organically and traditionally in Shropshire but even he does not have a Horkey. His wife remembers tales of Horkeys gone by when harvest home meant eat, drink and be merry. As the fiddle played those celebrations included passing a corn dolly around the table. When the fiddle stopped, the one with the dolly ('the neck') chose a partner to take out into the darkness, hence the word 'necking'. That too sounds like a tradition ripe for revival.

My search for a modern-day Horkey seemed doomed to end in failure. I need not have worried as I raised the subject with the sensible, responsible, traditional Hugh Oliver-Bellasis. Hugh did not let me down. On his family estate the Horkey is still alive and well. It has changed, to cater for modern times and tastes, but it is still flourishing. 'When I was a boy we held it in the village school for all the workmen. There would be beer, pickle and a roast. The blacksmith would sit there with a gigantic meat fork with half a gallon of pickle and it would all disappear, washed down with beer. He was a big man whose shadow would cover the two of us'. Hugh's Horkey of memory was an all male affair with beer and beef disappearing in large quantities as a fiddle played. Now things have changed: 'We thought it was too chauvinistic and the ladies have been brought in. All our staff now go to a local hotel in October. People are more important than things. Those land-owners and farmers who forget their people forget their business. None of our businesses would exist without our people'. This year the Horkey was slightly different on the Manydown Estate – the harvest supper was held in June, before harvest, to celebrate the 80th birthday of Hugh's mother.

By coincidence I have just discovered two other farmers who still enjoy a Horkey: Roger and Cherry Clark in Suffolk. I should have realised long ago that they would celebrate the end of harvest. They have Suffolk sheep, Red Poll cattle and their Suffolk Punch horses are still used to pull the binder and cart the corn. The Clarks disprove, by example and results, virtually everything said by the agri-business brigade during the past 40 years about traditional farming. Labour is not a problem at harvest time as thatchers wanting the straw help with the shocking, carting and stacking. Threshing time is remarkable too; then Roger has so many volunteers that he does not become involved; it leaves him with more time for his pack of blood-hounds. With a farm like this it is inevitable that the end of harvest is celebrated with a blow-out at a local pub.

Sadly, even here, on our small East Anglian family farm, our Horkey has disappeared. John, my brother, and senior partner, simply forgets to put it on the calendar. As on so many farms throughout the country it has just quietly slipped away. Instead I have started a new tradition and one to be recommended to all those who have let their harvest supper disappear. I have started a Horkey at breakfast time – a gigantic harvest breakfast.

The day after harvest I stay in bed until nine. Friends who have helped, or who have just happened to drop in during harvest, then come round for a gigantic fried breakfast: eggs, sausages, bacon, beans, black pudding, tomatoes, mushrooms the size of a plate and potatoes, all piled high. On top goes that prize of breakfasts past, fried bread, crisp, tasty and full of fat, every heart consultant's nightmare. In years gone by my father had variations of such a breakfast every day, but by 12.30, 'dinner time', he had burnt it all off. Today such a feast is special. I don't burn it off: it takes a week to smoulder away. The harvest breakfast is washed down with something special too, a bottle of Laurent-Perrier champagne. I have three years' worth left, then I will have to go in for The Laurent-Perrier Award for Wild Game Conservation again.

This year harvest started in a very odd way. I was high up in my roof-top study, writing words of wisdom, when this strange, yet familiar sound came wafting through the window. It was distant, both in feet and inches, and in memory. Then I spotted it; the local thatcher was cutting his field of Wigeon wheat with an ancient binder, for the benefit of good thatching straw. It brought back memories of my childhood, of horses and carts, the clattering of the binder; sheaves, shocks and the stacks being thatched to keep out winter weather. As the area of standing corn dwindled, rabbits would run the gauntlet of the guns for cover. We would find leverets; larks sang over every field and the drifts and farm tracks were bright with wildflowers and butterflies. These memories are not the fanciful, romantic wanderings of a faltering mind, they were reality.

Other men would come to help with the shocking; the self-employed and men such as Charlie, who slept in his signal box at night and worked on the farms and gardens during the day. I wish somebody would draw a map showing where 'shock' and 'stack' become 'stook' and 'rick'. With today's built-in idiocy of academia there could even be a PhD in it for somebody – although they will have to move fast as the last of the old land-workers, like the last of the old soldiers, are quickly fading away.

The best time for me during the binder harvest was simple: dinner time and tea time. Then my mother would appear with a willow basket and out would come sandwiches, squash, crisps, Worcester apples and the occasional bottle of Woodpecker cider. In the heat of the afternoon it was so peaceful sitting in the shade of the elms at the edge of the field. Today it seems part of a different world – a more sane world.

Latterly we had a Horkey – a family feed, with Charlie, still moonlighting, and his wife Harriet. It was a big feed, with ham and pie and still Woodpecker cider. My mother, a farmer's daughter, chapel, and almost TT, somehow saw cider as part of harvest. The generation before, my grandfather always bought a barrel of beer for harvest. One year he was worried by the fact that the level was dropping fast before harvest had started, so he laced it liberally with senna pods. Surprise, surprise, it was a teetotal chapel-goer who was first taken short.

It was the generation before that when Horkeys were still in their hey-day. Men with scythes, their 'July razors', would run their blades along the cobbles of the farmyards to announce their arrival looking for work. They would scythe through hay time and harvest and then the celebrations would really begin. In her classic 400 pages of local tradition *Cambridgeshire Customs and Folklore* (1969) Enid Porter caught the last memories and stories of harvests gone by. In almost all the local villages the last load of harvest, the Horkey, was decorated with branches. The workers would ride on top, often with the 'Lord of the Harvest' and his 'Queen', sometimes a man dressed up as a woman. There would be cheering and singing followed in the evening by wild harvest Horkey suppers: beef, beer and plum pudding followed by singing and dancing. It was the real world, the world described by Thomas Hardy and Henry Fielding. Robert Herrick too caught the mood of harvest home in verse:

Come Sons of Summer, by whose toile,
We are the Lords of Wine and Oile:
By whose tough labours, and rough hands,
We rip up first, then reap our lands.
Crown'd with the ears of corne, now come,
And, to the Pipe, sing Harvest home. . . .

The importance of harvest and the joy of Horkey were experienced over many centuries, with both gradually fading away in the first part of this century. Right up to the beginning of the Second World War the old celebrations could still be found. But the end of the war heralded a new age, the age of technology, industry and urbanisation, all on a scale never before experienced. Farming, the countryside and all rural traditions have taken a back seat. People shopping in supermarkets, who view everything from bread to sausages as a 'product', no longer recognise harvest, yet alone understand it.

But we must restore our traditions and keep them going, if only to educate the vast urban majority. Two years ago, I started the Countryside Restoration Trust, and part of our aim is to raise the awareness of the general public to farming and the countryside. We want to raise the awareness of some farmers, too. To do this we have even started some new celebrations to bring the countryside and its importance and enjoyment back into the country calendar. We are anxious to start a Countryside Sunday, simply to stimulate the interest of Christians and non-Christians alike into the wonders that can still be found around us in almost every parish. It was started this year in my local village church, with an address by Sir Laurens van der Post. We hope to make it an annual event, the Sunday on or after St Barnabas's Day (June 11th), the traditional start of hay-making, when the countryside is in full bloom.

On the first Saturday of December we have a barn dance with a rural theme, just to raise our jollity levels, ready for Christmas.

Next year we will have a Horkey too – not just for those who have worked on the harvest, but for all those who have seen it, and who enjoy its fruits. It will probably be the night before the harvest festival, so that we have somewhere quiet and cool in which to recover.

32

On the Scent

ða

I like my nephew but he has one fault, he tends towards political correctness. I can understand the problems of today's young people of course, with pressure from the media, trendy educationalists and social manipulators telling them what to think, say and how to behave. Consequently my nephew speaks, thinks and looks like a student straight off the 1990s brainwashing production line. He wears an earring, he believes hunting should be banned, he is a vegetarian and he wears a leather jacket. Please don't write to me asking for an explanation of how vegetarians square their beliefs with wearing leather. I don't understand it either.

He is not alone in this seemingly contradictory behaviour. Some time ago I visited an anti-hunting rally to see for myself the sort of people who believe that foxes are creatures of peace and perfect living. There was leather everywhere, worn by people eating veggie burgers, sucking soya and wearing the uniform of the Animal Liberation Front. It is a pity, for without the social pressure and urge to conform many of them would show signs of intelligence; with a little help they could even become individuals.

I took Edwin back to his college in Plymouth the other day. Just before dusk, half way between Chipping Norton and Stow-on-the Wold, I said 'We are in the heart of real hunting country here, Ed – it's part of their tradition and heritage and they should be allowed to get on with it'. His reaction said it all. His brain muttered silently: 'Here we go again. I'd better not say anything as I am getting a lift'. Then, suddenly the traffic slowed, the road was full of horses and hounds. It was the Heathrop Hunt 'going home'. There were pink, green and black coats; the horses were mud splattered and steaming, as were the hounds; a huntsman with side-whiskers, even better than mine, blew a blast on the horn and there were real Cotswold accents with a fine rural burr.

It was picture postcard stuff; a picture that will stay with me for a very long time. Here was an image of tradition still alive and well – a world in which internal combustion, political correctness and urbanisation were absent, for a day at least. It was a breath of pure, clear English air and I breathed it in with thankfulness. 'That was good, Ed', I said, as we drove back into reality. 'Yes, I really enjoyed that,' he replied, much to my amazement. If only more people could see hunting in its true rural context. But I fear it is too late; the urban take-over of all aspects of our lives is almost complete.

As I have said before, I do not hunt, I like foxes and I have kept foxes as pets, but at the moment there are too many about; they do much damage to wildlife and are a constant menace to free-range farm stock. Hunting to me seems the least offensive and cruel way of reducing the numbers without trying for extermination. I suppose the main objections are based on the Basil Brush syndrome; most suburban people give wildlife human feelings and reactions 'how would you like to be chased like a fox?'. The questions should be reversed: 'How would you like to eat raw meat and live under ground?'. 'If you were a fox would you kill and maim far more than you need?'. To compare human behaviour and responses with those of animals is simply absurd.

Another problem with the Basil Brush syndrome is that it is highly selective. The one animal that is exempt from its benevolence is the rat. Wherever the rat appears it is murdered, with no quarter given. It is hounded with dogs, assaulted with clubs and most inhumane of all, it is poisoned, causing a slow, painful death, out of sight and out of mind. When and if hunting is banned it will be the triumph of prejudice over reason, distortion over truth and political correctness over freedom. I have no vested interest in hunting whatsoever; in fact it would be more convenient for me to be an 'anti', but responding to the facts truthfully is more important to me than convenience or fashion.

In my view the hunting of a wild animal over open country is far less offensive than cruelty to domestic animals. That is why I simply do not understand the Co-op. As a sign of political correctness it stopped hunting over its land several years ago, yet its own headquarters admits that each year up to 1000 calves from Co-op farms are sold on the open market to end up in veal crates. To me that is simply hypocritical. If the Co-op, or for that matter William Waldegrave, want to prevent their calves going for veal, all they have to do is keep them for a month and start them on solids – the calves are then spoilt for veal and have to go for beef.

Over recent years the RSPB has been taking a much more sensible attitude on predator control and now controls crows, magpies and foxes, to protect its more vulnerable species. Imagine the chaos caused just before Christmas when a lady visitor opened her car boot in the Minsmere car park (Suffolk) and released a family of full grown fox cubs. She apparently thought they would be 'happy on a nature reserve'. It is almost beyond belief that anybody could release a family of carnivores on a nature reserve famous for its rare ground-nesting birds (avocets, terns, waders and wildfowl). Alas this is the fantasy world in which we now live. The RSPB called in the RSPCA to live trap (in the circumstances it could do no other); the neighbouring gamekeepers sought a more permanent solution. Peace has now returned.

33

Fit For A Prince

>●

I have more good news and bad news this week. The good news is that Prince Charles dropped in for a cup of tea the other day. The bad news is that I was out. It's not just bad news, it's a tragedy. I have this problem with meeting royalty and Prince Charles in particular. A few years ago I had to meet him at Balmoral to talk about the wildlife of the Highlands. I arrived on the wrong day. Last year, with amazing skill I managed the right day, but got to Highgrove late. Every single caravan in the Cotswolds was on the road directly in front of me, travelling in convoy at 20 mph. Now this has happened; Prince Charles arrived to see the work of the Countryside Restoration Trust and I was miles away watching sheep being rounded up by dogs. Sadly there was no alternative. I couldn't cancel 'One Man and His Dog' and so I had to miss the Royal visit.

Although I was sorry, as I regard Prince Charles as one of the few voices of sanity in an increasingly insane world, I need not have worried. The visit went well with the Prince being hosted by my good friend and CRT Trustee Gordon Beningfield, the painter.

HRH was shown the hay meadow, the new hedges, the damage done by the NRA, the lot – well, not quite the lot – they forgot the brand new otter dropping, left almost in tribute; its smell of bloater paste was superb, the Prince would have found

131

it a wonderful experience. He was shown too, some old hedges nearby, full of their ripe wild harvest. They were, I am assured, a wonderful sight in the sunlight of early autumn with their abundance of hips, haws, wild hops, sloes, blackberries, spindleberries, crab apples, buckthorn berries and strings of scarlet bryony. What a contrast to those other hedges up and down the country shaved into berryless conformity by farmers following fashion instead of tradition and common sense.

After the tour, mostly on the Royal foot, the Prince returned to the farm for tea. It must have been a special occasion for there my father wore a matching pair of shoes, unlike the occasion of Mr Gummer's visit a couple of years ago when he wore one green wellie and one black.

As usual, Prince Charles left a swathe of admirers in his wake. The fact is that on environmental matters HRH talks sense, sympathy and the language of ordinary country people. If only the politicians and the farming establishment would listen and follow suit.

The most important question asked by Prince Charles during the course of the visit was, apparently, the whereabouts of my dog Bramble. This is not as strange as it may appear, for although Bramble might seem dishevelled, even scruffy, in fact he is very well connected. He was bred by the retired head keeper at Sandringham, Monty Christopher. Monty is, and was, one of the best traditional gamekeepers; he is a wonderful naturalist, he

can sing folk songs, play virtually any instrument that can be plucked (most appropriate for a gamekeeper), he can tell a good tale and drink a yard of ale (even after October 1st – 'M Day' – Madness Day).

He designed Bramble to look like a small deerhound. Using a Norfolk lurcher bitch and a Bedlington terrier dog standing on a large book, he managed to breed what is possibly the most attractive dog in Britain.

Unfortunately the Prince missed Bramble; he was with me. If he had stayed at the farm I would have been filming 'One Man Without His Dog'. In retrospect, Bramble's absence was a good thing. For the whole of the summer he has been plagued with fleas; big fleas, little fleas, black fleas and brown fleas. They have been all over my house; they have even driven me from my bed, something that has never happened before. I swear there was one so big that it vibrated the mattress every time it took-off and landed. I used everything possible to get rid of the invasion: powder, sprays, flea collars and flea drops. All they achieved was to make me cough; they seemed to thrive on the stuff. No sooner had I eradicated one swarm, than Bramble nosed up to the farm cat or another lousy dog and brought another black battalion with him. Finally, in desperation, I phoned the council's flea, wasp and rat man. The next day they were still jumping, playing leap-frog and crawling up my trouser legs. So I had a plain choice, let Bramble stay at home and pass the fleas on to Prince Charles, or take him with me and give them to all the leading sheepdogs and shepherds in Britain. I chose the latter and Prince Charles had a lucky escape. The strategy worked: on returning home after filming, Bramble was totally flealess. I hope the next series of 'One Man and His Dog' will not be ruined by sheepdogs stopping for a scratch on the outrun and shepherds wearing flea collars.

For reasons of political correctness and conservation purity some people will not accept that some gamekeepers, particularly the older ones, are excellent naturalists. The absurdity of this was demonstrated to me earlier in the summer when Gordon

Beningfield wanted to paint a skylark's nest. Sadly I hadn't the time, nor had he, as searching for a lark's nest with eggs can be like looking for a needle in a haystack. I asked several conservation bodies if they could oblige. They all drew a blank. Then, by coincidence I bumped into the Game Conservancy's keeper, Malcolm Brockless. Within four days Gordon had his skylark's nest.

A reader in Kent tells a superb skylark story. Her father told of a little Cockney girl who went out to the countryside on an outing from London. She saw a skylark hovering over a field singing and said: 'Cor, look mum. There's a sparrer up there and 'e can't get up and 'e can't get down and 'e's 'ollerin' fit to bust'.

34

Time for a Tup

೩

Time flies, it's the Tupping Season again already. Not for me, I
hasten to add; ladies of assorted age, shape and colour can all
visit me in perfect safety. I'm referring to my sheep. Alarmingly,
this year's tupping time almost came early, when a neighbour's
hot-blooded young ram kept breaking into my little flock of
assorted virgins, ladies and matrons. Surprisingly, for girls so
well bred and behaved, several of them showed signs of wanting to respond to his coarse, tongue-flicking advances, in a most
unladylike way. Consequently he had to be forcibly ejected on
several occasions. I think the randy ram had been reading
Christopher Curtis's famous verse:

I'm a well-endowed ram and I've got where I am
By performing my act right on cue.
When it's time for a tup, I just line 'em all up
And shout 'Volunteers? Ewe, ewe and ewe!'

Counting sheep, as everybody knows, is a dangerous task,
particularly just after dinner in the hot, hazy weather of summer. Several times I had to pinch myself to stay awake, particularly when there seemed to be one extra – then its time to
double check, count the legs and divide by four or count the ears
and divide by two. Yes, I had an intruder. My neighbour had a
small herd of Texel rams next door, surely one of the most

unattractive sheep ever bred. So the quickest way to spot him was to call them all up and look for the ugliest, the squat, leering Number 10. 'Come in number 10 your time is up'. The best way to catch him was to throw some sheep pellets down and jump on him. Who needs a sheepdog when they are trained to the bucket? Then, once seized, I would roll him over and drag him by the back legs, down a ditch, over a fence and he was back with the boys. Leaving me exhausted at the bottom of the ditch smelling like a randy texel ram.

On my next visit, sure enough, there would be one extra sheep: leering, squat Number 10. As soon as I left the scene, he simply flopped over his sheep netting fence and walked straight through my electric fence as if it wasn't there. To counteract the activities of this walking woolly expression of sexual harassment I doubled the number of posts in the fence, making the three strands of electric wire tight and impenetrable. It worked; on my next visit he had flopped over his fence as usual only to be confronted by a high voltage ram raider deterrent. He would walk up and down outside, looking in, every so often placing his nose on a wire. With a fizz and a flash he would perform a double-somersault, before coming back for more.

Finally, I chased him into the nearby ditch and jumped on him. The AC/DC had evidently given him more energy than usual as he charged off through brambles and stinging nettles with me on his back. I hate to imagine what a small group of people were thinking as I went galloping past. Finally the beast collapsed in a heap with me on top. I rolled him over his fence, back into his field, and lay bleeding, stinging and exhausted at the bottom of the ditch, still smelling of ram. As I recovered somebody out for a walk approached me: 'What's happened?' she asked. 'I've been attacked by an enraged sheep,' I replied. Number 10 had learnt his lesson and he didn't get out again.

My little flock is a mixture. I have black, white, brown and mottled. The blood line, if that is what you care to call it, is Suffolk, Jacob, and yes, ugly Texel, in varying measures. I suppose almost a third of my breeding ewes are black, or blackish.

This means I have a problem. I learn that in Liverpool it is now politically incorrect to teach small children 'Baa, Baa, Black Sheep'. Pathetic, isn't it? Instead the poor, deprived dears (deprived of their childhoods) are being taught 'Baa, Baa Woolly Sheep'. You guessed, 'Baa, Baa Black Sheep' is considered racist. I suppose on the other hand 'Snow White and the Seven Dwarfs' is racist for choosing Snow 'White', and what is more, it makes fun of the disadvantaged. Perhaps in Liverpool it should become 'Snow Person and the Seven Vertically Challenged'.

Anyway, my problem is that as I do have black sheep, what do I do when we are worming or lambing? Two of my old geriatric footballing friends help me with my shepherding. I hate to think how they would reply to 'Denis – stop that one, the woolly one'. Or 'Mick, stop it, that not white one'. Alternatively of course the politically correct educationalists of Liverpool should be taught that the simplest description of a black sheep, is to call it a black sheep. I have just been delivered with a new great nephew; I am going to buy him a bumper book of traditional nursery rhymes – just as long as it contains the unexpurgated version of 'Baa, Baa, Black Sheep'. The second book, if I can find a copy, will be that wonderfully written and illustrated book 'Little Black Sambo' – if anybody seriously thinks the book is 'racist', then they must live in a very small, sad, distorted world.

Much more worryingly I have just discovered that I have been discriminated against by the BBC. The long, leggy blond that does the television Lottery Programme on a Saturday night, a programme that I have never seen, gets almost as much for one 15-minute programme, as I get for a whole series of 'One Man and His Dog'. Surely this is sexist, leggist, and blondist. I hope the politically correct of Liverpool will rally to my support.

Incidentally, the new series of 'One Man and His Dog' starts next Saturday night. It is up against Jim Davidson, as funny as a dose of laryngitis, 'Blind Date', and 'Noel's House Party'; at last I will be able to watch quite happily, although with my current weight, it does mean that for part of the time Mr Blobby will be on the two BBC channels simultaneously.

According to BBC insiders the birth of Mr Blobby was interesting. A BBC floor-manager sketched the idea on the back of an envelope. Of the fortune the pathetic creature has brought in, my mole claims that the BBC gets 50%, Noel Edmonds's production company gets 50%, the floor manager receives 0%. Good old Mr Blobby.

35

Picking and Pecking

❧

It has been a wonderful year for woodpeckers; we have been flush with them. One day in the summer I had a family of green woodpeckers and great-spotted in my garden at the same time. The greens were on some dead elm suckers, deliberately left untidied for such an eventuality, and the great-spotted were on my plum trees. As my garden is quite small I am sure the density must have broken some EU Woodpecker Directive. I have no idea what the collective noun for woodpeckers is; probably a 'chisel'.

It was a welcome sight. It was about 2½ years ago that I welcomed the laughing call of the green woodpecker back into my parish after an absence of 30 years. Their demise then coincided with the disappearance of many attractive species of bird and beast, thanks to DDT and its variants. The outlawing of these chemicals came just in time, not only for the woodpecker, but also the otter, the barn owl, the sparrowhawk, etc.

But hearing the 'yaffle' of the 'rain bird' again was only the beginning. Would the return of the green woodpecker be permanent and would it breed? The youngsters in my garden gave me part of the answer.

Denis is a friend of very long standing. I first played with him when I was three, and we are still playing together today. His 'mobility of employment' has meant that he has travelled much further in life than I have. I live 15 feet from where I was born, Denis has migrated a full three miles from his birthplace. He is a country boy through and through; he's an expert in a dark brown liquid that is still sold by the pint, he can grow a good leek and he played village football until he was 50. At 53 he is still 'signed-on', aiming to stagger on as 'sub' when the weather improves.

This year Denis noticed green woodpeckers too, and located a nest at the bottom of his garden. That is where I thought my visitors came from – until last week-end. We were then joined by an even more widely travelled villager, Mick; he was born four miles away. We went to put up the last kestrel and owl boxes given to the Countryside Restoration Trust by the Hawk and Owl Trust. The kestrel box was due to go into an old willow tree by the brook. We located a suitable spot, but once up the ladder Denis had to think again, for there, half way up the tree, was a hole with a chamber behind it: another green woodpecker's nest.

The return of the green woodpecker has given me much pleasure. As much of East Anglia is so treeless I believe that the bird has been helped by set-aside and the presence of ants. On the CRT's Holt Field we have taken the land between the brook's meanders out of production, a fact loved by the hares, English partridges and goldfinches, in addition to the 'yaffles'.

My love of the green woodpecker has just led me to do something entirely out of character: spend money. I foolishly visited the preview for an auction of 100 original paintings by Charles Tunnicliffe. The pictures were old commissions for the RSPB and the Society decided to sell the work at Sotheby's, in London, to raise money for its work in Wales. It raised about £275,000.

Oh dear, the pictures were amazing, with far more life and colour than I had expected, and, oh dear again, there was a green woodpecker flying over snow-covered branches. Tunnicliffe has long been a favourite artist of mine, ever since I saw his woodcuts in *Tarka the Otter*. I had never been to a picture auction before and a still small voice inside said: 'You must buy the woodpecker'.

It was strange, going to a Sotheby's auction. It is not the usual activity for a poverty-stricken English peasant. I needn't have worried, for I immediately met my old friend and fellow CRT Trustee, Chris Knights, the well-known Norfolk peasant, parsnip grower and 'Survival' film-maker. He was after a picture of his beloved stone curlews, which he failed to get. 'You're looking smart,' he said. 'Nice binder twine!'. I had forgotten my coat pockets were open and still bulging with string from feeding the bullocks that morning. He was too polite to mention the Suffolk Punch dribble stains on my shoulders, given to me recently by a cart horse while visiting Roger Clark, one of the last Suffolk peasants. We peasants stick together.

There was obviously a lot of money at the auction, and I thought I had no chance – but then I had a cunning plan. The fat wallets were in full cry and most pictures were fetching well above the recommended price. Then came the woodpecker. The cunning plan came into action (it is far too cunning to reveal here) and I began bidding with what appeared to be a plastic lollipop. It seemed to work and I got my beloved bird well within the forecast value. But now I have another problem. Where do I put it? The walls of my hovel are already full, and what do I live on until Christmas? It seems as if I will have to join Bramble on his Bonios, or even Bonio gruel.

This year everybody has become familiar with the work of Tunnicliffe, as his work is featured on stamps commemorating the 50th Anniversary of the Wildfowl and Wetland Trust. This is strange, as the WWT was founded by the late Sir Peter Scott, himself an accomplished painter of wildfowl – so why is the Royal Mail using Tunnicliffe? It is rather like going to a concert to celebrate Vaughan Williams and listening to Beethoven.

A film company is currently behaving in an even more peculiar way. It is making a film of Thomas Hardy's classic Wessex novel, *Tess of the d'Urbervilles*, in *Yorkshire*: 'Eh oop Tess lass, what's grieving thee?'

36

Fatter, Rounder and Older

&

I have no idea how long it will take me to recover from Christmas. As a result I have already made one New Year's resolution and that is to never again stand on the bathroom scales. I suppose it doesn't really matter, for in my present state, even if I stood on them, I wouldn't be able to see them. I think the problem is genetic; on both sides of the family there are, and were, little fat, round men who got fatter and rounder as they got older, and now it's happening to me. The basic shape is rugby ball, with Wellington boots at one end and hair at the other.

Life is so unfair: there are people I know who eat and drink every day as if tomorrow is their last. They remain thin, fit and ravenous. I simply look at food and proceed to expand on all fronts and so Christmas is a most difficult time. I have never knowingly refused bread sauce, brandy butter, mince pies or sloe gin, and so, as a result, all my trousers, shirts and jumpers appear to have shrunk. If I was a BSE free bullock, as all ours are, I would be considered a 'good doer'.

I thought something even stranger than an expanding waistline had happened to me on Boxing Day. At the meet of the Cambridgeshire Foxhounds, I was approached by a total stranger who greeted me with: 'It's nice to meet you Mr Bugg'. 'Mr Bugg?', I queried. 'Yes, you're Old Bugg. You can't fool me.

I've seen yer picture in me book.' I explained to him that there were no Buggs, or even Fat Old Buggs in my family – we were totally Bugg free. Then, all was revealed: the mischievous John Humphreys, the infamous countryman, raconteur and racketeer (racket as in 'din': trumpet-playing) has produced a new book 'More Tales of the Old Poachers'. It is well up to Humph's usual high standard, but there, on the back cover, is me, complete with added earring and spotted neckerchief. Inside there I am again, looking even uglier, drawn by that outrageous artist, cartoonist and non-shaver, John Paley. The pictures do indeed accompany a story about Old Bugg, a notorious poacher and ne'er-do-well. For anybody else who imagines that they see Old Bugg trying to live his normal life – the name is Page – I have never poached in my life, I do not wear an earring and I have never chased the Old Bugg around a tree. Messrs Humphreys and Paley should remember one simple rule: he that laughs last laughs longest.

I had hoped that my weight problem would be sorted out by now because of two important events. Just before Christmas the skies opened and the frost came. There was one 'Come lovely morning rich in frost' after another and the skates came out: fen skating is a wonderful way of keeping fit and fighting flab. The earth was hard as iron and the farm puddles froze solid. After the third night I phoned Edward Dow, in the fens, to see if he had flooded his skating field as normal. 'I haven't been able to, Robin,' he replied, 'the ditches are empty and the river level's way down'. He confirmed what most people seem to have forgotten: the drought is still with us. Things may be damp, but that is due to low evaporation, not rainfall, and unless heavy rain comes soon there could be serious water shortages next summer.

Last year's drought was not much of a problem because the year started with water tables not just high, but spilling over. If another dry year follows on and a deluge or three do not happen soon, then a summer water shortage, poor crops and wildlife at risk will be inevitable consequences. It is so obvious to those of us with our feet in the fields that the water companies should be telling households to take care *now*.

My other enjoyable slimming aid is the CRT annual Barn Dance. I love barn dances as it doesn't matter if you get all the movements wrong and a steady exchange of partners means that everybody is included. It was a theme party – VE and VJ Day – which meant there were air raid wardens and American servicemen present and women wearing politically incorrect, moth-eaten furs. Some sad people arrived as sandbags, one came as a black-out: she was totally invisible in the dark. There was a rotund, transvestite Winston Churchill and another came as a complete airfield, covered in hangers (the coat variety) model planes and carrots for the night-fighters.

Star of the evening was the redoubtable Sid Kipper who gave his services entirely free. Sid is a visionary/warbler from the centre of the known universe, Trunch, near Cromer. Yes, there is such a place and Sid has twinned it, not with Vienna or Venice, but with Barnsley. Any potential visitors can get there by following the trans-Norfolk Highway, also known as the B1145. Despite the volume of the applause and cries of 'More', Sid finally stopped almost exhausted; apparently the Norfolk Kippers are not known for their durability. However, he has promised to return in 1996, complete with his musical sieve and walnut shells.

37

A Shot in the Foot

૨৯

As a non-hunter, shooter and fisher, it can be a depressing experience watching a minority of country-sportsmen trying, with much success, to shoot themselves in the foot. My backing for country sports is simple; country sports carried out responsibly have a positive effect on conservation, and a wide range of creatures, plants and landscapes benefit directly as a result. But that is not all; although I do not participate myself, country sports are still part of my rural heritage and culture – my inheritance. They are part of the social fabric of rural Britain and are of immense importance to many rural communities.

In addition, the involvement of ordinary people in field sports is an expression of freedom; democracy is not just about 'the will of the majority', it is also about respecting the freedoms of minorities, and those practising country sports today are a minority. If they are victimised and their sports are banned, then they are not the only ones to suffer: our democracy will suffer and the fundamental concept of individual freedom will be under attack.

As an outsider I have said all this before, but increasingly I ask myself, 'Why should I bother?' By defending country sports I expose myself to attack and misrepresentation, while at the same time some country sportsmen seem reluctant to defend themselves or stick together.

Much of this stems from the current political position. Many field sportsmen seem to assume that hunting is doomed, yet if they keep their heads down and play along with Labour's strange band of environmental policy 'persons', everything will be alright in the end for shooting and fishing.

Sadly, nothing could be further from the truth. As sure as night follows day, if hunting does go, then shooting and fishing are next on the list. Various animal activists openly admit that their agenda is long, and these days, wherever certain pressure groups go, a number of ego-polishing, publicity seeking MPs are sure to follow. For those who doubt this, it has always seemed odd to me that hunting has been the chosen object of attack. As a conservationist, if I wanted to embarrass the field sports lobby I would find it far easier to attack fishing first and shooting second. Hunting would be the last as it is the one country sport whose ways are almost the same as nature's. The fact that the activists have so successfully addressed the issues in reverse order can only be attributed to the clever use of emotion rather than reason – the hounds in full cry after their quarry; the political envy and anger of the unspeakable in pursuit of the uneatable and the general ignorance of a largely uninterested urban majority.

At the moment various organisations are trying to bring fieldsportsmen together as a united front. But at the same time some of the assorted fat sprats in fishing's hierarchy are keeping their sport at an arm's length. Some shooters are taking a similarly short-sighted view. The fishermen should pause to think; the anti-fishing arguments are already there, the antis know them and have them, complete with photographs and film. They are simply biding their time.

Hunters are attacked for not eating their quarry. How many coarse fishermen eat their quarry? Even some game fishermen are now putting back their catches; this means that the anglers are fishing for one thing only, something that is totally alien to all antis; they are fishing for *pleasure*. 'Pleasure', according to most antis, is something that must never be experienced at the expense of bird or beast.

Then of course there are numerous other issues that the fisher-men have made little effort to address seriously. There is the problem of discarded hooks and lines injuring and maiming wild birds; there is litter; there is the disturbance to other wild-life caused by fishermen fishing during nature's breeding sea-son; there is the cruelty of live-baiting; there is the eco-illiteracy of those fishermen agitating to abolish the closed season. I could go on. So are there still anglers who believe that their sport is safe and will not come under attack? In my view, if hunting goes, fishing will go too, sooner or later. The threat is there, obvious and growing.

All this makes shooting even more vulnerable, and again the antis already have the evidence. From Scotland, as I write, come horrific stories of geese being shot over decoys, not in ones and twos for the pot, but in hundreds, simply gunned down and buried in mass graves. Some groups of Italians and Belgians are shooting geese in such large numbers and leaving them, that they could get exactly the same sort of enjoyment from shooting clays. The root cause of course, is the financial greed of the shoot organisers. It is unacceptable; it is immoral and it is not sport.

Believe it or not I went to a partridge shoot in September with a film crew from Anglia Television, somewhere in East Anglia. It was a driven partridge day, with mainly reared partridges. On one drive hundreds came over, the sky almost blackened. 'That was a good covey,' the shoot owner informed us. It wasn't a covey, it was a cloud. The gun at our end, right in front of the camera, missed the 'fun', as the partridges were further down the line. So what did he do to amuse himself? He started shoot-ing pheasant poults, out of season, that could hardly fly. If I had been the shoot owner I would have ordered him off the land and banned him. But he stayed; there were no cross words and I suspect that he had paid a fat cheque for his day's 'sport'. For-tunately the camera crew did not film him. But if it had been filmed and shown, some field sportsmen would have com-plained of media 'bias'. In my view it was a case of crass stu-pidity and ignorance on behalf of the shooter.

Almost as bad, I was told the other day of a group of Cypriots who own a shoot in Southern England. Before the start of the season they had pheasant poults thrown out of the release pen in order to sharpen up their aim. With this sort of nonsense going on, do shooters really believe that their sport will be safe under a Labour Government?

I accept that these people are not typical, otherwise I would be unable to defend field sports. But what about those shooters who claim to be responsible and who state that shooting and conservation go hand in hand, yet at the same time are demanding the return of the curlew to the quarry list? What a nonsense; what irresponsibility; what a public relations disaster. I am a useless shot, yet I could hit a curlew; I am reliably informed that they taste like mud and their numbers are steadily falling, so why make an issue of getting them back on the quarry list?

As a conservationist I could make a case for putting the Brent Goose on the quarry list – but the curlew? It is another shot in the foot – own goal – call it what you like, it is shooters giving shooting a bad name and making the task of the antis even easier.

I want country sports to survive. But please, all those who hunt, shoot and fish, stand together; carry out your sports responsibly and throw out your renegades before it is too late.

38

Gone Away

ɞ

The Cambridgeshire Harriers recently held their Point to Point races, the first of the season. Instead of being a typical, happy, exciting event, it was a sad occasion – for the Cambridgeshire Harriers no longer hunt and soon will have disappeared completely.

Every year since I can remember they have met in the village in a field behind the Post Office. It has always been a friendly meet and even many of us who do not hunt would attend, to see the horses and hounds and renew old acquaintances; the sherry and hot sausage rolls were also part of the appeal.

As political correctness has crept into the countryside and more and more people have lost their links with the land and rural tradition, I have often been asked why, as a conservation-ist, I attend the meet. The answer is simple. I choose to. Hunting and all its social off-shoots are part of rural life, part of its heritage and culture. In addition it has always seemed to me that hunting is the field sport that is closest to the ways of nature; as such, if hunting's opponents were really concerned about 'per-ceived' cruelty, then logically they should be opposed to fishing and shooting first. Sadly, the hunting debate is not about logic, it is about prejudice, misunderstanding and a fundamental sepa-ration from nature. I have hunted three of four times as a jour-nalistic exercise and the hunt I initially rode with was the

Cambridgeshire Harriers. The first thing I learnt was that if you ride a small horse directly behind the backside of a large horse, the digestive system and extractor fan of the large horse leave much to be desired.

Riding in a donkey jacket, to match the horse, I was made welcome and at every turn, Hugh Gingell, a local farmer and joint owner of the Harriers, was at my side to ensure my safety and well-being. In fact Hugh and Betty Gingell *were* the Cambridgeshire Harriers. They bred and showed horses and were famous throughout the equine world, but their biggest love was hunting, with the hounds kept on the farm.

Hugh died last year. He was a quiet, knowledgeable, humorous man – a gentleman. In recent years, after his riding days were over, a mutual friend would bring him over to our farm in the spring. He wanted to see our Country Gentleman's sponsored hay meadow and the cowslips returning. He was a modern farmer who had followed the line laid by MAFF and the NFU. In the spring before he died, in the accent of old Cambridgeshire, he stood in the cowslip field and said, 'You are right, Robin. We should all still have fields like this. We did too much to it'. I shall miss him in the Spring this year, but the cowslips will still be there.

Last summer I visited the kennels. There were puppies and hounds keen for attention. Betty had decided to hunt on, at the age of 80. Then with the fall of the leaf, when the hunting horn should have been heard from the field behind the Post Office, all was quiet. Betty Gingell too had gone the way of all flesh.

It was a sad time. Nobody could be found to take on the hunt. The hounds looked out of their kennel full of eagerness – with nothing to do and nowhere to go. Slowly the horses went and the hounds departed in threes and fours. Now the kennels stand empty.

The funeral of Betty Gingell was a remarkable event. Her village church was packed, with an overflow and people standing in the aisles. It was a moving too with the wind and the call of rooks carrying the sounds of country into the church as the choir sang 'D' you ken John Peel'. The faces were of farming, hunting and country. There were people from huge country houses and small council flats. The congregation was a broad spectrum of country life with an age range just as varied.

Then it hit me. If hunting was banned, all these people, stalwarts of real country life and living in rural communities, farmers, accountants, vicars, farm workers and Justices of the Peace, would all become potential criminals, overnight. At a stroke their hopes, traditions and way of life would become illegal. It seemed incredible, unbelievable, all in a country that boasts of its freedom and tolerance.

Then another thought came; at least the horses and hounds of the Cambridgeshire Harriers went to other hunts in England, Ireland and France. If hunting is ever banned then there will be nowhere for the packs to go. Hounds will be put down in their thousands, cruelty will be administered in the name of compassion and individual freedom will be stamped on in the name of 'democracy'. Britain has become a sad, mixed-up place in which personal responsibility and belief is being swept aside by a mixture of political fashion and correctness.

A few weeks ago a former helper and follower of the Cambridgeshire Harriers told me how her life had been altered and saddened by recent events – her Saturdays were empty. She missed the horses, hounds, the people, and the hares too, which they rarely caught anyway. To help, I ignored a home game of Cambridge United and took her to a meet of the Cambridgeshire Foxhounds. It was almost too much: her eyes filled with tears and she wept. As we watched the hounds draw a cover between two villages, now known for their high intake of urban settlers and London commuters, a Volvo Estate car drove by at speed. A passenger lowered his window and screamed manically, 'You disgusting people!' Until recently my companion spent her spare time as a 'Samaritan'. I wonder why that made her disgusting?

39

Brass Monkeys

ða

As I have written many times before, I love cold weather, but
when the recent thaw arrived I was relieved. It meant instant
escape, not from the 'inconvenience' of snow and ice, which
caused me no inconvenience whatsoever, but respite from the
continuous torrent of inane prattle served up by our news and
weathermen, women and persons. Don't they know that it is
supposed to get cold in winter? Don't they realise that the rest of
northern Europe survives without the hysteria which accom-
panies every snowflake that falls on Britain? What is wrong with
these people? I suppose it is yet more evidence, if any more were
needed, that this country is totally urban dominated, out of tune
with the seasons, nature and reality.

On the farm water froze. So, we simply kept one tap flowing and watered the cattle through a length of garden hose.
Immediately after use it went back close to the fan-heater. If
the electricity had gone off we would have lagged the pipes
and kept the tap running slowly. If the water had been cut off
we would have let the cattle into the frozen meadows to
drink from the brook, which was flowing too fast to freeze. It
was all as simple as that – no crisis, not panic, no problem. In
fact the so called 'freeze-up' was a Sunday School tea party
compared to the winters of 1947 (which I can just remember)
and 1963.

During the recent sorry apology for a freeze, not only was I warm, I was hot. Wearing long johns, jumpers and a woolly hat is not an affront to being male. I prefer to have no image and keep warm. While taking part in a local radio programme, a female member of the Church Synod proclaimed that the problem with cold weather these days was 'that nobody wears long johns anymore'. Alas, I had to roll up my trouser legs to show her. Why is it that members of the Church Synod always get it wrong?

Even in my house I have been warm, thanks to woolly jumpers; wool is warm – that is why 40 million British sheep wear it. Several non-wool wearers called to see me during the freeze; they hung their coats in the hall and joined me in the living room. After just a few minutes they retreated back to their coats; yet with my various layers I was steaming. When I checked the temperature I have to admit that even I was shocked: my living room was a balmy 50 F. I have raised the temperature by 10 degrees since then, to prevent any crazed social worker calling on me to claim that I was 'disadvantaged' or 'underprivileged'. In addition of course, I must have been breaking an EU home heat directive.

The fact is that on the whole we keep our houses and offices much too warm in winter. Nobody should be indoors in shirtsleeves; we should save energy, have lower room temperatures and wear vests, jumpers, woolly socks and hats. During a cold spell my woolly socks only leave me when I'm in the bath.

Perhaps the BBC's great conservation watchdog programmes should investigate the enormous waste of heat and energy in British offices during the winter. They ought to sneak-film people in shirtsleeves inside over-heated work-places, with snow outside. We shall never see such a revelation, as the BBC is one of the worst offenders, including the Countryfile offices.

The separation from nature and reality is now being made worse by an obscure Tory backbencher. Apparently this Mensa candidate wants to change winter time through a Private Member's Bill; Greenwich Mean Time, our natural geographical time, will become Central European Time. Someone should pluck up the courage to tell the poor man that we are not in Central Europe, nor even the Heart of Europe; we are on the Western edge of Europe surrounded by water – an off-shore island. Perhaps it is the Tories' lack of geographical knowledge that has led them to become so entangled in the Euro-farce, and persuaded them to give nearly all our natural fishing grounds away.

GMT in winter is most beneficial to those of us who work on the land and who have livestock. An hour of daylight in the morning is worth two at night, but as usual our requirements and views are unimportant, after all, we only produce food. It is at dawn when frost and black ice are at their worst; presumably our suburban MPs will only realise this when the number of morning accidents increases. As usual, various figures have been quoted to show that more accidents occur in the evening, but the manipulation and presentation of figures can prove anything. Hence our Euro-friends continue to tell us of the great financial advantages of belonging to the EU, even though our current account with Europe is in deficit.

One set of injury figures for last year has proved interesting. Incredibly, four people were injured by their underwear. Just before Christmas I almost became the fifth. I left for the Black Hole at such speed that I accidentally put my long johns on backwards. In the good old days one p in London got you precisely that. Now it costs an outrageous 20p. You don't 'spend a penny', but 'two florins'. My contortions were so great when I couldn't find what I was looking for, that I almost injured my back. I will take much more care in the future.

I am getting a lot of chaffinches on my bird table at the moment. Strangely, this little bird also shows how urbanised we are becoming. In southern Britain 'chaffinch' is correctly pronounced 'charfinch', as the bird was once commonly found pecking in the chaff of winter farmyards. Now, few people seem to know that chaff was, or is, or how to pronounce it. It is surely time we began to separate the wheat from the chaff?

40

The Fat Man Sings the Blues

෨

I could not believe the cover of a *The Shooting Times* the other week. What had happened? The whole page seemed to be devoted to a plump, well dressed gentleman sporting a cap and a pipe. What could this mean? Was it an advertisement for John Brocklehurst's excellent country clothing or was it recommending a Saga Holiday for the elderly in cold climes? I looked again – it was neither; it was none other than John Humphreys who had apparently won a prize.

It is not often that I am overcome by a bout of envy, but I was at that moment. In the past I have come second in the Laurent-Perrier Wild Game Awards; I have also come third, but I have never won first prize – yet all my neighbours seem to win the thing outright. First there was Will Garfit with his famous gravel pits, forcing me into second place. Now it is the redoubtable John Humphreys coming from nowhere to scoop this year's main prize. What makes the matter worse, so many admirers want to see the great man receive his award that I cannot even get an invite. To be perfectly honest, it is not the money I begrudge, it is the champagne. Why should a man, however great, receive a case of champagne when he is so obviously out of shape and condition? For anybody rude enough to suggest that I am a smaller version of the same design I have to state quite categorically that my problem is genetic.

I first heard of John Humphreys many years ago when he started writing for the *Shooting Times*. I sat up when I read that he was a teacher – a politically incorrect teacher. A teacher who shot and fished, and wrote for the *ST*, when the rest of his profession seemed obsessed with 'Gay rights', banning golly-wogs and Enid Blyton and refusing to supervise sport because of its 'elitist' nature – village football elitist? Although I had never met the man, I immediately took to John Humphreys.

Then came books and I first met the flesh – much less of it then – 15 years ago when he was one of the guest speakers at a Literary Lunch in Cambridge. It was immediately obvious that he did enjoy his lunch, and so did the other diners, for although almost unknown, he easily matched the wit and wisdom of the other 'celebrities', Bernard Levin and Pam Ayres.

Since our first meeting I have got to admire the man as well as his writing. The most important thing about John Humphreys is that he's an 'ordinary bloke', like me and like you. His father was a vicar and Humph became a teacher: he had no land, no money and no privileges. His background was a country child-hood and his education was the wildlife and nature around him; from this came a deep love of fishing and shooting. His lack of land did not stop him, and as this interest grew, so did his knowledge of land management and manipulation. When he bought his small piece of Fen, Hunters Fen, he was able to put his theories into practice – then came the Lord's Ground Shoot.

The achievement is remarkable. A non-landowner and a non-farmer has taken on shooting rights and land management re-sponsibilities in East Anglia that puts some other landowners in the area to shame. That possibly is the greatest message to come out of this year's award: if John Humphreys can do it, and the landowners, the Greens of Soham, are happy financially for him to run such an environmentally friendly shoot, why can't more of the farmers and landmanagers in the prairie wastes of Cambridgeshire and Huntingdonshire follow suit?

But of course all this is only part of the story; if the Laurent-Perrier award was wider, to take in the whole public relations image of country sports, then John Humphreys would win that too. Since his first book 15 years ago, a whole stream of books have appeared, both informative and entertaining.

Then there is his trumpet-playing and after dinner speaking. Every other Thursday evening at the Longbow pub at Stapleford, near Cambridge, Humphreys blows his lungs out with Amadeus Boldwicket's Red Hot Peppers Jazz Band. The combined age of the band is about 2003 and the weight must be measured in tons – but it is all good entertaining stuff. And yes, Mr Humphreys indulges in movements and sounds that resemble the rut of the wildebeest; he calls it singing.

There is still more. Although this man of many meals and talents took early retirement from teaching several years ago to concentrate on his writing and shooting, he still teaches. He takes groups of teenagers to see foxhounds, release pens and trout streams. He gets them to visit woods, farms and open fields, he tries to give them a crash course on the countryside – a course made necessary by the increasing urbanisation of rural Britain. In this he is setting an example that others should follow. Education is the only way to spread interest, understanding and tolerance among the urban majority.

Although I don't shoot, last year I saw the Lords Ground Shoot for myself at first hand. I was invited to become a beater. It was a cold, crisp day with the east wind blowing uninterrupted from the Ural mountains. The beaters and guns were all friends and if the evidence of my ears is correct, then the enthusiastic dogs had a most unusual range of rather coarse names. It immediately became clear why the shoot was now won the Laurent-Perrier Award as there was a whole host of wildlife, in addition to pheasants and partridges, because of the cover, spinneys, rough headlands and wetlands left for game.

In the pub, after a good day, Humph showed yet another side of his character. People kept talking to him about his books, this, that and their own escapades and each one was listened to with courtesy and smiles. This is not as easy as it seems. There is a famous story of somebody travelling hundreds of miles to see the late Henry Williamson to get him to sign a book. Henry Williamson opened the door and said two words – the second one was 'off'.

When a clerk retired from the Cambridgeshire Education Office after many years of service, he received just one letter of thanks and congratulations from Cambridgeshire's marvellous teachers – from John Humphreys. The Laurent-Perrier Award could not have gone to a more deserving winner.

41

A Skating Badger

It has been difficult to write this chapter; there simply hasn't been the time. I suppose too that I should be feeling pangs of guilt and shame, but I have no regrets: I have been skating every day and am proud of it. I have another confession to make too; skating has coincided with the arrival of Badger for our annual hedge-laying bash. To make up for lost time in the past he set aside two whole days this year. Alas, on day one we started work at 3.30pm, just in time for a neighbour to bring us tea on a tray. The second day was written off completely. Within productivity like this I suppose we should follow the example of those who rule us and ask for a substantial pay rise.

The skating has been strange this year. The frost almost crept in unnoticed. Under cloudy skies it was windchill that brought in the freeze. On several mornings my lawn stayed green with not a single trace of ice, yet the ground was cold and hard and the cattle drinkers were frozen solid. That meant only one thing: a trip into the Fens to see if the ice would bear.

Much to my relief, Bury Fen, the traditional skating field, had been flooded and much to my surprise I was the only person there. It is an amazing feeling to glide at speed, without effort, over the ice. It gives a sense of freedom and movement that people of my shape and condition rarely experience. Being at the western end of the Ouse Washes the setting is made even more remarkable by the wildfowl. As I skated, wigeon and pink-footed geese flew over and then, as I rested against the branches of a willow, a small group of Whooper swans came in to land, calling conservationally as they dropped down. They seemed to think that they were landing on water and slid chaotically on touch-down, trying desperately to use their tails as brakes.

Bramble loved the deserted ice and ran with me excitedly. I have much in common with my dog; at 13 he is still behaving like a puppy. His favourite moment on the ice is when I stop sharply and he keeps going out of control.

As the week went on others appeared until last weekend crowds were on the ice. Even Badger ventured on, staggering about on skates that he had bought at a second-hand shop for £10. He hadn't been on skates for 30 years and it showed. His dainty, hesitant steps and waving arms reminded me of the courtship dance of a flamingo – although I have never seen a flamingo crash into the sitting position with its legs tangled in reef knot.

Races followed and even some fen pensioners were covering 1½ miles in only five minutes. Although the tradition of fen skating is strong, as in so many countryside sports there are few youngsters coming up to replace the old-timers. The drainage madness of the last 40 years is part of the problem. Before the diggers and draglines had their way virtually every lowland village had its water meadows. After just three nights of a reasonable frost the shallow pools would freeze solid and half the village would be out on skates. Sadly, those water meadows have gone, as have the traditions of wildfowling and skating that went with them. The other problems stem from the urbanisation of society itself. People no longer link freezing temperatures with fun and sport: they think of discomfort and inconvenience which is an entirely urban way of looking at a cold winter.

The other problem today is that many people equate ice with 'danger'. Ice is not a problem – it is the lack of understanding or respect that is the problem. As with so many things, the most accurate guide is the one used by country people for genera-tions: 'If the ice bends it breaks; if it cracks it bears'. When I go onto ice I usually carry a Scandanavian device given to me by my Swedish sister-in-law – many Swedes carry one – it consists of two wooden handles with a steel point sticking from each one. If the worst happens then it is possible to grip the good ice with the metal points. Unfortunately hardly any of these simple gadgets seem to have crossed the North Sea.

As the number of skaters increased, so did the antiquity of the skates and skaters. One man at over 80 was still skating, albeit erratically. He could remember one winter years ago when the only water to freeze was at the Cambridge Sewage Farm. The National Fen Skating Championships were held on sewage, without an Environmental Health Officer on Euro-Directive in sight – those were the days.

On several mornings a smallholder appeared with his entire family, four children and his wife. His skates were screwed into old boots onto which he had fitted iron brackets to support his ankles. With three acres and a cow he was an interesting man possessing an unusual view of history. 'Take a look at the shape of my wife's head,' he said, almost proudly. 'That's a Norman head, as if she got off the boat yesterday. You look at most of the Fen farmers – they've nearly all got Norman heads. After all these years the Normans still own nearly all the land. It can't be right'. With grievances like this the Irish problem seems almost recent.

His view of history was not altogether accurate. I have distant relations farming in the Fens. Their ancestry certainly does not stem from the Norman Conquest but from Scottish prisoners of war, brought down to England to drain the Fens. Their plight must have been desperate, but at least their arrival brought in some much needed genetic diversity. Fenman in kilts competing with Normans! It's strange how skating on a winter's day can give a totally fresh view of history.

42

A Common Sense By-Pass Operation

☙

Life has been quiet without John Seldom Glummer. Since his departure to the rarified atmosphere of the Department of the Environment he has become almost a Saint. Environmentalists love him; on occasions he appears to talk sense and those dim and distant days at MAFF, closing down slaughterhouses, tolling the death knell of the small farmer and pulling the plug out of our fishing fleet seem like a far off nightmare.

However, last week our paths crossed again when I was invited to the Black Hole to hear about the wonders of the National Forest – which indeed seems like a sensible idea. St John told us that 'the people' wanted a green and pleasant land and they supported environmental policies. Then came a classic piece of Gummerism. He told us that when the Republicans were elected to the Senate and Congress, they took their seats pledging to remove all environmental constraints. Since then they have had to do a complete U-turn, as they found that many of those wanting environmental safeguards voted Republican. A few sentences later he followed this up with a reference to the Newbury By-Pass. How 'democracy' must be followed and the road – a piece of environmental madness if ever there was one – must go ahead. Even forgetting the monumental myth that road enquiries bear any resemblance to democracy, dear John, and the rest of his Cabinet cronies, seem unable to link the American experience with our own: that a large number of the Newbury protesters, the ones providing food and comfort for the tree-dwellers, are card-carrying Conservatives actually living in Newbury. I know, for although I haven't ever written about the Newbury By-Pass, until today, various Newbury residents have already written to me. Alas the Conserve went out of Conservative years ago and the Tory leadership is too blind to see it.

The biggest irony in all this of course is the fact that the new Lib/Dem MP for Newbury seems to be as environmentally illiterate as the Tories. So another myth explodes – that the Lib/Dems are 'green'. I am not against cars. I love my Daihatsu Fourtrak, but the car should be serving us, not enslaving us. The answer to the Newbury By-Pass problem is simple: a tunnel, as it should have been for Twyford Down. Why can Hatfield have a successful tunnel and Newbury cannot?

The church has slipped up over internal combustion, too. When last year the CRT started its Countryside Sunday, we felt a special day was needed to promote the countryside, as most Christians, and non Christians, seem unable to tell the difference between a cowslip and a cowpat; yet these same people can recognise a Saab from a Honda at 400 yards. In other words people are familiar with man's creation but have lost their link with God's creation. Now the Bishop of Coventry has emphasised the point by parking cars in front of the altar of Coventry Cathedral to celebrate the 100th birthday of the car – the golden calf of 1996 is called a Daimler.

I was discussing the whole concept of celebrating centenaries in church with my old father the other day. We decided that to celebrate the 100th anniversary of the condom, the Bishop of Coventry should use his crook to tow a condom-dispensing machine up to the altar before a congregation of social workers, feminists, pimps and trendy members of the Church Synod.

Mr Gummer's main achievement since moving to the D of E has been his Rural White Paper. For its content and intent I give him 8 out of 10. For its impact on the countryside we must wait and see. When he introduced his effort to Parliament, the most important document on rural affairs for decades, our MPs showed their true commitment to the countryside; the House of Commons was virtually empty and poor St John was almost talking to himself.

The Countryside Restoration Trust sent a submission for the White Paper; among those of our suggestions totally ignored were several concerning roads. One of the greatest menaces of our age is traffic speed. Although one teenager dying from 'ecstasy' turns the media into a frenzy of excitement, the 3500 who die on our roads annually, the great majority through mindless speed, create no interest whatsoever. The answer is simple. Each parish should have three or four people trained to use a radar gun – local junior school children recently became competent in half an hour. Then, to relieve our courts the fines should be administered by County Councils. This would solve the problem of speeding within a month and free the police to combat other areas of crime.

Filling stations were our other concern, ignored by the White Paper. Why, in beautiful countryside and picturesque villages, are garages allowed to look like large Lego buildings, complete with bunting, flags and advertising hoardings as large as cricket sight screens, all ablaze with light? When I pass a pub with a picture of a wagon and horses outside, I know what is for sale inside. So why are garages allowed to stand like monuments to 20th Century ugliness, bad taste and planning madness?

I have got John Gummer on the brain. The other day I even dreamt about him. I was sitting in my armchair, a mug of tea on one arm, listening to the cricket. I drifted off to sleep. Suddenly St John was batting, hitting the ball towards me. I swooped to run him out, and threw the tea all over my trousers. Alas, the story is completely true.

43

Fieldfare Fantasy

ॐ

At last the redwings and fieldfares are here in hundreds, even thousands; in fact I can never remember seeing so many redwings. Each autumn and winter I look out for them but for some reason, as the nights lengthened and cooled and the berries on the hedgerows glowed in the setting sun, last autumn, the birds did not come. In October I made a short visit to Scotland: normally the valleys are full of these Scandinavian visitors moving South and the peregrines, already full, kill, simply for the fun of it. This year in Scotland I did not see a single flock. I began to worry that a great natural disaster had befallen them, then, all of a sudden towards the end of January, I saw my first large flock of fieldfares. The weather turned cold and I need not have worried. Since then I have never seen so many of our visiting winter thrushes.

The sight of so many birds feeding on the wild harvest of the hedgerows has been truly wonderful. Our large hedgerows have given them food and shelter during their time of need – reward enough for the loss of production caused by having hedgerows and not wheat right up to the field edges.

Perhaps that is why our fieldfares and redwings looked so numerous – they homed in to our hedgerows, as most of the other farms in the area have few hedges. Almost all those that do remain are trimmed in the summer so destroying all the traditional winter food for birds.

I do not understand the current farming fashion of cutting hedges out of season – in the summer. Recently students at Shuttleworth Agricultural College in Bedfordshire, gave me some answers. 'We cut our hedges early to make the farm tidy;' 'Tidy hedges are a sign that you take a pride in your farm;' 'Right after harvest is the proper time to cut your hedges'. It was a sad experience listening to such environmental illiteracy coming from our farmers of the future. Give me wild hedges and redwings instead of tidiness any day. Farming with wildlife in view is responsible farming. It really is time our agricultural colleges took a broader view.

Of course some farmers argue that leaving hedges causes economic loss and such losses cannot be tolerated. In today's farming climate that is nonsense. Prices are good. Subsidies are better and any farmer who claims that he cannot afford to leave some of his farm for wildlife must be a very bad farmer.

I still call the fieldfare by its local, country name of 'fulfer'. In fact I have never heard my old father call it anything else. Strangely none of my books of birds' names mentions 'fulfer' for fieldfare – evidently the authors didn't come to Cambridgeshire. My father still uses several other old country names regularly: the 'saw sharpener' (great tit), 'hedgie-bet' (hedge sparrow) and 'screech owl' (little owl).

After my reference to the 'charfinch' a few weeks ago a reader from the South West came up with another perfect country name for it – the 'copper finch'.

Not only do I disagree with out of season hedgecutting but I also don't see the sense in out of season lambing. Winter lambing seems strange – the ewes and the lambs have to be fed and in cold snaps heat must be provided too. I prefer to wait until the grass is growing and the sun is getting warm and lambing is more natural.

April the first is the date when I am to get my first lamb. Last tupping season, for the first time since I started keeping sheep, the tup failed to get round to all my young ladies. I was astonished – either he was a very tired old tup or I had two exhausted elderly matrons. I have to admit that the borrowed Suffolk tup seemed alright. On his return home he was repeatedly charged head on by two young pretenders but he saw both off without a sign of a migraine. It is amazing how this ancient and wild behaviour still takes place in an animal that has been domesticated for centuries.

Fearing my two ewes might soon have to become mutton I took them to the farm to give them extra food. After a week I thought my stock of sloe gin was getting the better of me. One night I heard bleating. There were not two sheep – but seven. It was not the gin: one of the ewes had presented me with triplets, while the other had given me twins. Then it dawned on me. My barren ewes certainly were not barren; my neighbour's terrible Texel tup, the one that had walked through the electric fence in the summer, had had his wicked way with them after all. The only way I ever want to see a Texel ram again is on a plate with plenty of mint sauce.

The breeding habits of our animals have caused a lot of trouble lately. The other day a reader enquired what had happened to Snowdrop, our Middle-White sow. It is a sad tale. Before Christmas she was put with the boar; she appeared to get on well and, after doing her duty, she almost seemed to smile. Then she did something she had never done before, she dropped down dead – still with a smile on her face. Perhaps this sort of behaviour should carry a Government Health warning. All Texel tups please take note – it could happen to you.

44

Go With The Flow

ॐ

An angry woman appeared on my doorstep the other morning; I have to say that fortunately such a scene is not a regular occurrence: 'The NRA are at it again,' she panted, 'can't you stop them?'. My heart sank. Fortunately her fear and anger were misplaced. It soon became clear that the men were not from the NRA's notorious 'dredge and drain gang', but from the more positive 'go with the flow brigade'. In other words the NRA had arrived to make good the damage it had done to The Countryside Restoration Trust's efforts to recreate water meadows.

With the sterling support of a large number of *Telegraph* readers the Countryside Restoration Trust bought 40 acres of land alongside a tributary of the Cam two and half years ago. Then, last year, after much time, energy and money had been spent on restoration work, including raising the water level of the brook, the NRA 'drained' downstream of the project and virtually all our water drained away. Initially suggestions from the NRA's 'humour' department blamed drought, but after an independent environmental assessment (of the type that did not occur for the Newbury By-pass) Dr Nigel Holmes agreed with us, that the damage had been caused by the NRA's over-enthusiasm.

Fortunately the NRA has accepted the report and it is now making good the damage. It has dug out two deep pools along the Trust's stretch of brook and used the gault clay taken to make obstructions in the bed itself. We hope that this will lead to deeper water the whole year through. One of the obstructions is diverting water around the revamped meander that thanks to the mad drainage work dried out completely during the summer. Later on in the year the NRA is to carry out more remedial work on the actual stretch of brook it damaged and so a year later than intended, the CRT's restoration work is back on course.

In addition, as an indication of good faith, the NRA has also carried out some pollarding of old willows for the Trust. This time the work was carried our well and sensitively. Some landowners pollard willows in long lines, changing the landscape suddenly and completely. We have lopped some and left some, so that there is a mixture of trim trees and old sprawling trees. It means that those pollarded will be able to renew themselves, while the old ones will continue to provide the holes and crevices for tree creepers, green woodpeckers and even swarms of bees, and the half hollow trunks will remain ideal for resting foxes and otters.

I have to say too that the CRT is grateful to John Selwyn Gummer for his support; when he heard the original news he really was Seldom Glummer. The whole incident has also been an interesting test for the CRT. Some conservation charities have

suggested to me that in the real world it is impossible to criticise large bodies, whether they be government, quangos or big business – 'you have to remember, you might want them as donors'. From day one we decided to be honest, to describe things as they are. Consequently, by 'going public' we understand that the NRA's drainage procedures have been overhauled, for the benefit of all landowners, farmers and conservationists alike. Similarly last year when we named specific farm chemicals that may be influencing skylark survival (again with the DTs support). Some farming and conservation groups, with generous agri-chemical sponsorship, appeared shy to follow suit; yet some of the resulting dialogue between the CRT and chemical companies, with support from the game Conservancy, has been invaluable.

Recently CRT members again came from all over the country to plant more hedges. These were not the usual thorn hedgerows for marking boundaries and keeping in livestock – they were flowering and fruiting hedgerows planted entirely for their landscape and wildlife values. They contain crab apple, wayfaring tree, rowan, wild cherry, blackthorn, etc. as well as clusters of hazel and wild rose. In addition to these it is hoped to add an odd bullace and a medlar; then, once the small trees and shrubs have become established we will plant the entire length with honeysuckle, hops and old man's beard. In 15 years' time it will be exciting being a butterfly or a bird along those hedges; will they grow fast enough, and will I live long enough for the introduction of the dormouse?

One of our tree-planters was a lovely teacher from Henley. She told us a depressing tale about the urban values that have invaded her area. A neighbour complained to her recently: 'I am being woken every day at dawn by a bird singing'. 'What is it?' she asked. 'I have no idea,' he replied. 'It's black with an orange beak'.

Worse still, a *Telegraph* reader has just given me a mail order catalogue: 'McCord – design by mail'. Anybody with £19.99 to spare can make an astonishing purchase: 'Strictly for the Birds!

Look forward to some new visitors in the spring with these charming painted wood birds houses with their authentic corrugated roofs. Choose from the pitched roof Sparrow box or sloping roof Lark box'. Yes a 'lark box' – now we know why lark numbers appear to be declining. They have given up nesting on the ground in open fields, they have gone to live up trees in 'lark boxes'. Residents of Henley beware.

Another horror story has also just arrived. A farmer near the A1 in commuter land was told: 'Would you keep your sheep quiet on Saturdays and Sundays please. I work in the city all week and come to the country for peace and quiet at weekends'. Apparently the noise of this motorised rat-runner driving through the village five days a week to join the A1 was permissible.

45

The Bitten Bittern

ॐ

The fashion in conservation at the moment is reedbeds. They are a good fashion to have as they are attractive places, with much wildlife potential. Consequently a variety of bodies and private individuals are creating new reedbeds and the RSPB has funded an excellently produced book on how to manage them (*Reedbed Management*, £14.95 from The Lodge, Sandy, Beds) – so, everything in the bog, swamp and marsh would appear to be rosy. There is something however that puzzles me: one of the intentions of all this reed is to provide ideal conditions for one of our rarest birds, the bittern, the booming bittern. But I have seen no warnings that reedbeds also provide ideal conditions for one of our most common predators, the fox. In other words, in a few years' time any passing bittern tempted to drop into one of these new reedbeds could well become a bitten bittern. Indeed, if it is a passing female responding to the love boom of an amorous male, it could become a smitten bittern bitten.

During last summer I met one of Britain's oldest and most respected biologist/conservationists. In fact I respect him so much that I will not give his name. He was telling me with enthusiasm how the reedbeds at Wicken Fen were to be extended and that he hoped this would bring back the bitterns. I was rather alarmed at this, because I prefer living bitterns to bits and pieces of bitterns outside a fox's earth full of hungry cubs. A friend tells me that Wicken Fen is heaving with foxes, crows and magpies and most years a marsh harrier tries to breed but its eggs are eaten by crows. When he took this up with a member of the National Trust, owners of Wicken, he was told; 'That doesn't matter, Wicken is mainly a botanical reserve'. In other words, bye, bye biodiversity.

I pointed all this out to the learned reedbed-lover and added that creating habitat for birds without controlling predators was rather like getting a beehive and filling it with some bird or beast that regards bees as a special type of pudding. It seemed to me that in next to no time any landing bittern would become a fox's supper and by creating these conditions conservationists could be doing more long term harm to the bittern population than good. He disagreed: 'Oh no, foxes are not a problem at Wicken, in fact they do some good, they take the Canada geese off their nests and stop them breeding'. In other words the foxes would take the Canada geese and leave the bitterns. It seemed a most extraordinary theory and also an example of the astonishing tunnel vision some conservationists seem to develop to avoid facing the realities of predator control.

Many wildlife wardens and gamekeepers along the Norfolk and Suffolk coast, some already managing reedbeds, have absolutely no doubt what will happen to bitterns returning to reedbeds where predators are not controlled – 'they will be scoffed in five minutes'.

The issue clearly shows the difference between the practical working conservationist and the conservationally correct wildlife policy-maker. At a recent meeting in Norfolk I asked an employee of the RSPB how he would protect the bitterns. 'They'll be quite alright,' he said 'where they nest the water is too deep for foxes'. A warden with mud on his hands and water in his waders had a different view: 'Foxes love reedbeds. They find them warm and inaccessible to enemies. They will find a dry bank to have their cubs on and create havoc if left alone. In fact the nearest type of nest to the bittern is that of the greylag goose. Foxes have them off their nests as quick as winking. I don't allow any to get on this reserve. I'm not allowed to say this publicly of course because it's not official policy to admit this sort of thing – but if you want the birds, bitterns, avocets or whatever, you have to control the predators. The gamekeeper does it for his pheasants. We do it for our birds'.

To the practical countryman and conservationist all this is obvious: so why won't the main conservation bodies admit that the only way to get a maximum variety of species on a bird reserve – biodiversity – is to control (not exterminate) some predators? Strangely, the RSPB already knows this to be true and on some of its reserves there are wardens operating almost as gamekeepers. When it bought its Abernethy Reserve in Scotland several years ago the RSPB stopped controlling foxes and crows and numbers of the magnificent capercaillie and blackcock crashed as a direct result. Recently they have been eliminating crows and foxes and last year they succeeded in having the best survival of blackcock chicks in Scotland.

Yet I have read no reports of this good news in any RSPB publication or Press release; apparently it has been classified as 'research'. Fortunately not only does the RSPB have birds, but it also has 'moles', keen for the full story to get out. From this the conservation message is clear and simple: habitat management by itself is not enough; good conservation equals habitat management i.e. the planting reedbeds, plus population management, the control of predators. Only then will the bittern not get bitten.

Recently my good friend Chris Knights, farmer and wildlife film-maker, whose film on the stone curlew was shown the other day on Anglia TV, had to drop out of a talk. His place was taken by one of the country's best wildlife photographers, David Mason, a gamekeeper. When the new man was introduced to the Bury St Edmunds RSPB Local Members Group – yes Suffolk again – he was described as a 'game warden'. 'Gamekeeper' was just too much. I wonder if Lady Chatterley would have joined the RSPB?

46

Mad Cows and Barking Ministers

ஐ

The possible link between bovine spongiform encephalopathy (BSE), mad cow disease to you and me, and Creutzfeldt-Jakob disease (CJD) in humans has apparently come as a complete surprise to Douglas Hogg, the Secretary of State for Agriculture. The sight of his inept television performance last week was not Nero fiddling as Rome burned, it was Hogg bumbling as a large section of the rural community and the rural economy were sacrificed on the altar of official incompetence. How could this link between BSE and CJD be sudden or recent? I asked a leading veterinary scientist about the link two years ago. He was in no doubt: 'There is almost certainly a link. The disease is not even new, it has been around for years. I have stopped eating some cuts of beef. I will have nothing around the head or spinal cord. I am amazed that you can still buy oxtail in butchers' shops and there is no way that I would eat a beefburger – there's no knowing what goes in them. I eat steak and roast, properly cooked. There's no threat in that'.

My vet was just as convinced at the same time: 'I've stopped eating beef altogether. We don't know what the link is but we know it's there'. Since then his taste buds, or gluttony, have got the better of him and he is eating beef once more, but again only good cuts well away from the brain and spinal cord.

177

So if I could get this information, where were Mr Hogg and Mr Dorrell (the equally incompetent Health Minister) getting their information? The answer is simple; they were consulting their own Ministry the 'mafia' of MAAF, a department known for its secretive nature, its incompetence and its lack of practical knowledge about sane, sensible farming. Indeed the present regime at MAAF has master-minded the present situation in which traditional farming, rearing animals and crops sympathetically with nature and the countryside are finding it increasingly difficult to compete with those who have turned their farms into factories. On those monstrosities, intensive production is the 'efficient' aim, much to the satisfaction of MAFF, the NFU and the supermarkets – agriculture's deadly triangle. It has to be said that customers too have played their part in this fiasco. They have chosen cheap, mass-produced food without apparently realising that 'cheap food' is bought at the expense of hedgerows and wildlife (which are deemed inefficient) and humane farming systems, which are considered 'sentimental', 'backward' and primitive. The farming establishment has taken the 'culture' out of 'agriculture' and turned it into 'agribusiness'. BSE is only the first well publicised harvest from this stupidity – there are almost certainly others on the way. Of course, BSE is almost certainly present in the intensive systems on the Continent. A farmer who trades in both Holland and France claims that it is there already, they simply do not recognise it as BSE and call it by another name.

Richard North, the well known food safety expert, sums up the current situation well: 'There is not a word in the English language to describe the utter incompetence of the Ministry. Everything that could be done wrong has been done wrong at every single stage in the crisis. It should be remembered that BSE is not a new disease. This epidemic began in the early eighties. What has been done since? It was first described in 1912 as 'cattle scrapie'. The other astonishing thing is that everybody is assuming that the cause is cattle feed, yet it could be a combination of things'.

Here our politicians and the media have done us no favours. While the ministers in charge have been gibbering incoherently, Harriet Harman, the shadow food minister, has been no better, simply trying to score political points. The media too have been alarmist, without any thought given to the damage being done to rural communities still producing good quality BSE-free beef. Part of the problem is that society is now totally urban dominated – particularly in Parliament, and the media. Genuine country people are almost an endangered minority and their views are seldom sought or listened to. Yet BSE is a rural problem and the causes, and the solutions are obvious to many of us living and working in the country.

Yes it is true that the feeding of offal up to 1988 could be a contributory factor, and it remains beyond reason how or why offal, 'meat', came to be fed to cows, herbivores, in the first place. Some say the problem started when the approved temperature for rendering the offal was lowered. The question has to be asked – why change a system that was working well with no health problems? Who pressed for the change, and are they still employed by the Ministry? But there are other likely candidates which need urgent investigation. For several years now – yes, especially since the early eighties, cattle have been compulsorily treated with organo-phosphate (OPs) chemicals for wiping out worms and warble fly. It is known that OPs can affect the nervous system, yet the treatment is to pour the highly concentrated toxic chemicals along the spinal cord of each animal.

On our small farm we have been worried about this for years but have been told it is the most 'efficient' – yes, that misused word again – treatment for warble. I suspect that MAFF will not condemn the use of OPs, or be honest about the links between OPs in sheep dips and illness in humans, for fear of attracting claims for compensation.

There are other unacceptable aspects of intensive cattle rearing that could contribute to BSE. The stocking levels on some intensive farms need to be studied. Some cattle never see green fields and are simply fed sileage with assorted chemical additives – again it is totally unnatural, but is it also unhealthy? Many people looking at the herds with BSE, particularly the dairy herds, and where specialist protein feeding takes place for showing, believe that it is a combination of these things that could lead to BSE. The nervous system weakened by OPs; the stress of high-density living; the over use of chemical additives for meat and milk production, and the legacy of the offal eaters – it is and always was a disaster waiting to happen.

Those now suffering from the collapse in beef markets and prices are the thousands of small farmers, family farmers, and enlightened farmers who rear their cattle in traditional ways, allowing them to graze in the summer, and feeding them on home-grown cereals and fodder in the winter. Most of them are totally BSE-free, yet all their animals, thanks to political and bureaucratic incompetence have been labelled a 'threat'.

Another message that comes through is the important part played by the organic movement; no BSE there. Yet they have received no government help, support, or subsidy. As in so many environmental and farming issues Prince Charles has played a vital role, and it is he who is leading the call to put the 'culture' back into agriculture. Yet sections of the media and Parliament itself are evidently too stupid to understand his contribution, best summed up recently by the midget-minded Ron Davies, MP for Caerphilly, who mocked him for 'talking to vegetables'. I had no idea that Prince Charles had spoken to Mr Davies!.

But it should be remembered that all this shambles has been paid for by one group of people – the British taxpayer, who handed over to farmers the massive total of £3bn last year. The irony in this is that in the apportionment of money, the large, rich, industrial farmers get larger, richer and more industrial, while the small, traditional farmers are still being driven from the land in real poverty.

It must be hoped that from the BSE scare will come a massive reassessment of the way in which British farming is funded.

Those who want to farm their fields and yards like factories should surely be like any other industry and receive no hand-outs. Those who farm humanely, with nature, and not against it, and who face up to their responsibilities for encouraging wild-life and attractive landscapes, for the benefit of everyone – they are the ones who should get long term financial assistance.

In the short term urgent financial aid must be given to those thousands of small farmers in the south west, Wales, the Lakes, Scotland, etc, whose lives and communities are being threatened by the current cock-up. Those herds with BSE links must be put down before any further damage is done, and most important of all, heads must roll in MAAF and the Cabinet room: Mr Hogg and Mr Dorrell should go the same way as that other agri-cultural incompetent of a few years ago, Edwina Currie. They should resign or face the sack.

47

A Yokel's Who's Who

ề

John Gummer: a man who has travelled a long way; from the Ministry of Agriculture to the Department of the Environment; from the Church of England to the Church of Rome, and in my writings, from total sinner, to almost saint. He appears to have developed a real concern for the environment; however it should also be remembered that he is still a politician.

IACS Payments: The Integrated Administration and Control System. It is an astonishing mechanism from the European Union. It pays farmers money for doing absolutely nothing. Eighty per cent of the money paid out in Britain (£1.6bn) is paid to just 20% of the biggest and richest farmers and landowners to help them become even bigger and richer. It was supposed to be paid as compensation for a projected fall in cereal prices. The fall did not come, yet the compensation is paid our annually regardless. The only phrase that I can think of, fit to print here, is 'how extraordinary'.

BSE: mad cow disease.

Edwina Currie: still out and about. Promisingly, she has lost a European election, and it must be hoped that she can encourage the losing trend into her Derbyshire constituency at the next General Election. She has become a 'writer' ('soft porn' rather than literature). She appears to be one of a growing number of MPs who seem to believe that politics is a branch of show business and that debates in the House of Commons should be treated rather like a television game show.

Jack Hobbs: one of the greatest cricketers the country has ever produced. His home was Cambridge.

Cricket: one of the greatest games ever invented. It requires, skill, flair and intelligence and so is not played in the United States of America. It crosses the boundaries of class and wealth and so in Britain it is not encouraged by politically correct school teachers who seem to thrive on divisions and prejudice.

Twyford Down: a motorway constructed through an environmentally sensitive area several years ago. It shows how the CONSERVatives at the time did not understand the meaning of their own name.

The Newbury Bypass: a new motorway actually being constructed as I write, through an environmentally sensitive area. It shows that the CONSERVatives of today still have no clear meaning of their own name.

Astonishingly, Newbury is ruled by Liberal/Democrats, who claim to be 'green' but who also want the road. Of course the biggest question is, how does anybody who witnesses a 'road enquiry' in action, believe that the system is either 'liberal' or 'democratic'?

Central European Time: the time used by people who live in the heart of Europe. Amazingly, some British people claim that they live in the 'heart of Europe' too, although it is obvious to most people, even Greek tanker captains, that we are on the Western edge of Europe. They want to use a time zone outside their natural, geographical zone. It must be hoped that they never want a close political and economic union with Fiji.

Miriam Rothschild: unlike Edwina Currie she is a remarkable, knowledgeable woman who has done an immense amount of work for the good of conservation in Britain, Europe and the world. The first Honorary Life Friend of the Countryside Restoration Trust.

Mr Douglas Hogg: Secretary of State for Agriculture. Often seen wearing a long coat and a silly hat. The most remarkable thing about him is that his father, Quintin Hogg, seemed unusually bright, articulate and able.

The Precautionary Principle: a principle signed by most developed countries guaranteeing that in all matters affecting the environment, caution would feature before opportunism, cash-flow or expediency.

Lack of Principle: a trait shown by most of those who signed the Precautionary Principle.

Mr Gordon Beningfield: he continues to be a very good friend of mine and the greatest living watercolour painter of our age. He is still Vice-Chairman of the Countryside Restoration Trust.

Mr Stephen Dorrell MP: on the grounds of taste and a desire not to waste paper, I cannot bring myself to write any more about MPs. The most reassuring thing about them is that the week after most of them retire, or get voted out, they become forgotten figures and we never hear of them again.